HOME OFFICE

Roadcraft

The Police Drivers' Manual

LONDON
HER MAJESTY'S STATIONERY OFFICE
1974

INTRODUCTION

This booklet, which succeeds former versions of *Roadcraft*, has been prepared by police officers and embodies the knowledge and experience gained through years of driving under all conditions.

Accidents, with rare exceptions, do not occur at any given times and places, but rather in widely scattered areas and at all times of the day and night. Comparatively few of these incidents can be directly attributed to any particular road feature or vehicle defect, but it is found that in nine cases out of ten the cause of the accident can be traced to the failure of the ' human element ' of the person or persons concerned.

The aim of the following chapters is to raise the reader's standard of driving to the highest possible degree of all-round efficiency. A vehicle can be a lethal weapon and, like a gun, it should be handled with care; the advice which follows is not intended to reduce the pleasure to be gained from driving, in fact the opposite is true, the more confidence and knowledge at a driver's disposal, the greater is his capacity for enjoying and taking pride in his driving. Furthermore, if the reader follows this advice he may one day save somebody's life—perhaps his own.

First published   1960
Second Edition   1968
Second Impression (*with amendments*) 1974

ISBN 0 11 340561 8

CONTENTS

CHAPTER 1

The Physical and Mental Requirements of a Driver

Object of Chapter

1. The object of this Chapter is to help the driver to realise the need for a high degree of physical and mental fitness in order to drive a motor vehicle according to the highest standards of skill, safety and consideration for other users of the road.

2. The law's requirements in this matter are not exacting and apart from specific cases an applicant for a driving licence or renewal of a licence is not required to undergo a medical examination.

3. Nevertheless, the average driver will find that he becomes aware of many contingencies through his ability to hear and recognise various sounds when driving a motor vehicle. Good vision, good hearing and a good standard of health all have an essential bearing on the power of concentration so necessary in present-day driving.

4. CONCENTRATION. The reactions to happenings seen and heard take place in the brain, which is the centre of control of all thought and action. To perfect control in any human activity, the ability to concentrate is necessary.

5. Concentration may be defined as the full application of mind and body to a particular endeavour, to the complete exclusion of everything not relevant to that endeavour.

6. The power to concentrate exists in everyone; but few can concentrate sufficiently to drive a motor car with complete mastery in all circumstances.

7. A high standard of concentration may be achieved by any driver by his own enthusiastic effort and by self-discipline. Self-discipline involves self-criticism, followed by an earnest endeavour to improve one's control of thoughts and actions.

8. With the aid of VISION, HEARING, GENERAL FITNESS and CONCENTRATION a driver will be able to exercise good JUDGMENT, which is the ability to distinguish between right and wrong, good and bad, safe and unsafe.

9. Moreover, he must be able to formulate a safe driving plan for every circumstance on the road, and then carry that plan into effect with DELIBERATION.

10. To do this his muscular system must be in good condition, for when driving, the movements of the limbs exercising control of the vehicle must be sure and accurate.

Driver Reaction Time

11. Driver reaction time may be defined as the time that passes between the moment a driver observes the need for action and the moment he takes that action.

12. The action may be to change the course of the car by steering, to make it go faster by acceleration or slower by braking. There may also be the need for a combination of steering and acceleration or braking.

13. Reaction time is of major importance when applied to braking. For example, a driver should be capable of reacting to an emergency stop by braking in two-thirds of a second. In that period, *i.e.* the period elapsing from his seeing the need to stop to the time he applies his foot-brake hard, the car, if travelling at 30 miles an hour, will have covered approximately 30 feet without losing any appreciable speed. This distance is called the THINKING DISTANCE and is referred to as such in the Highway Code.

14. The Thinking Distance will vary in three ways: (a) with the speed of the car; (b) with the physical and mental condition of the driver; and (c) with the degree of concentration he is giving to driving.

15. The ability to react quickly can deteriorate in several ways. Undue worry, fatigue, illness and the effects of alcohol and certain drugs are well-known causes of lack of mental and physical well-being.

16. To maintain his mental and physical condition, the average driver should live a normal and regular life and be moderate in all things; he need do nothing more.

17. Every driver should be aware of his reaction time and in the case of a person with an abnormally long reaction time it is recommended that some simple exercise should be taken to help co-ordinate the limbs and eyes.

Ten Commandments of Motoring

(1) KNOW THE HIGHWAY CODE BY HEART AND PUT IT INTO PRACTICE

18. The Highway Code is the road users' Bible and by adhering to its precepts you will do much to make our highways safe and more pleasant for all.

19. Issued under the authority of Parliament, the Highway Code sets forth rules by which all classes of road users are encouraged to govern their road behaviour. This fact must be borne in mind when giving advice to any member of the public on the proper use of the highway.

Drive according to the Highway Code and you will drive safely and well.

(2) CONCENTRATE ALL THE TIME AND YOU WILL AVOID ACCIDENTS

20. Concentration is the keystone of all good driving. It is a primary duty, but often a neglected one. Complete concentration will enable you to see and take notice of every detail. It is often the smallest detail that gives the clue to what will probably happen. If you miss such a detail, an accident, or at least an unpleasant experience, may result.

21. Concentration will also ensure skilful handling of your car and will prevent bad gear changes and late and fierce braking. It will practically do away with involuntary skids, which are usually caused by the locking of the wheels by fierce braking on bad surfaces.

Concentration assists anticipation.

(3) THINK BEFORE ACTING

22. The theory that a good driver drives automatically is a fallacy. To the uninitiated he may appear to, but the truth is that by continually concentrating and thinking he has raised driving to an art.

23. Every corner, bend, gear change, in fact, every driving operation, is a problem which, like every other problem, can only be solved by thinking.

24. A thoughtful driver carries out every operation or manœuvre in plenty of time and, consequently, is in the happy position of being able to accelerate from danger or stop to avoid it.

Think and avoid accidents.

(4) EXERCISE RESTRAINT AND 'HOLD BACK' WHEN NECESSARY

25. To 'hold back' is to follow at a safe distance a preceding vehicle which you eventually intend to overtake, until you see the road ahead is clear for a sufficient distance to allow you to overtake with safety. This will call for the utmost restraint, especially when driving a fast car, but never be tempted to overtake or carry out any other manœuvre unless it can be accomplished with 100 per cent safety.

26. By exercising restraint you automatically eliminate any tendency to impede other drivers by pulling in too quickly after overtaking, an action often referred to as ' cutting-in '.

A good maxim is ' *Whenever in doubt, hold back* '.

(5) DRIVE WITH DELIBERATION AND OVERTAKE AS QUICKLY AS POSSIBLE

27. Good driving continually calls for the making of quick and correct decisions, all of which must be carried out with deliberation.

28. Overtaking must always be accomplished in the minimum of time, so as to leave the road clear for others who may be travelling in the opposite direction, or behind you.

29. For the ' Don'ts ' often advocated in the text-books, substitute ' Deliberation '. A driver with a negative complex will sooner or later hesitate at the crucial moment, possibly with fatal results.

Deliberation eliminates uncertainty.

(6) USE SPEED INTELLIGENTLY AND DRIVE FAST ONLY IN THE RIGHT PLACES

30. It is not always safe to drive at the maximum speed permitted by law in restricted areas. In some circumstances such a speed is dangerous.

31. Where conditions permit it is best to drive at an even speed, as it assists in keeping traffic moving in an orderly and constant stream.

32. High speeds are safe only when a clear view of the road ahead is possible for a considerable distance. The speed in all cases must be governed by the amount of road that can be seen to be clear. Remember that at 60 miles per hour, a car travels a distance of 88 feet in one second. With many drivers, a second elapses between the seeing of an emergency and the applying of the brakes. Concentration and alertness are, therefore, absolutely imperative.

Any fool can drive fast enough to be dangerous.

(7) DEVELOP YOUR CAR SENSE AND REDUCE WEAR AND TEAR TO A MINIMUM

33. Car sense is the ability to get the best out of your car with an entire absence of jerks and vibration.

34. It entails smooth and thoughtful operation of the controls with hands and feet. This can only be achieved if the operations are carried out in plenty of time. Car sense adds to your safety factor as you will be in the right gear at the right time.

Good car sense increases the life of your car.

(8) USE YOUR HORN THOUGHTFULLY; GIVE PROPER SIGNALS; NEVER BLACK OUT HEADLIGHTS

35. Many motorists do not use their horn at all, some use it aggressively, others automatically and often unnecessarily. It is every bit as important that a person in front should be acquainted with your intentions as a person behind, yet many motorists who never omit to give 'signals' consistently fail to give audible warning of their presence.

36. Use the signals given in the Highway Code. An ambiguous signal is misleading and dangerous.

37. Flashing the headlights at night is a very efficient form of signalling. Dip them, but never black out (to black out is to switch the headlights off entirely, causing you to drive into a field of extreme darkness because the eye cannot readjust itself quickly enough after the glare of the headlights) unless driving in a well-lit area. There are occasions when the use of the horn may not be appropriate, *e.g.* between 11.30 p.m. and 7 a.m. in a built-up area (when it is illegal) or even by day when driving at a high speed on a motorway, dual carriageway or other fast trunk road (when it may not be heard).

In these circumstances an alternative means of indicating one's presence on the road may be necessary and flashing the headlights can usefully meet the need. It should not do more than that.

Give good signals and earn the praise of fellow road users.

(9) BE SURE YOUR CAR IS ROADWORTHY AND KNOW ITS CAPABILITIES

38. A defective car or motor cycle must never be taken out. To prevent this, check your vehicle.

39. Before attempting to drive a strange car fast, get accustomed to its controls, acceleration, braking capabilities and characteristics.

Car and driver must blend harmoniously to ensure good driving.

(10) PERFECT YOUR ROADCRAFT AND ACKNOWLEDGE COURTESIES EXTENDED TO YOU BY OTHER ROAD USERS

40. Roadcraft includes every phase of driving. It is something more than road sense. Many people possess the latter, but do not make the best use of it owing to lack of control, inability to use the road and position their car to the best advantage. A driver with good roadcraft knows how to avoid awkward and possibly dangerous situations. Good roadcraft not only prevents accidents but makes driving less arduous.

41. The Highway Code urges all to be courteous; but a good driver goes further and acknowledges the courtesies extended to him by every class of road user. By doing this, he sets a splendid example and does much to engender the spirit of chivalry so badly needed on our roads.

Courtesy is a great factor in road safety.

CHAPTER 2

The System of Car Control

Object of Chapter

1. The System of Car Control is the basis upon which the whole technique of good driving will be built. It must have a solid foundation, and any weakness in its structure, either theoretical or practical, will be evident in a driver's performance.

2. The object of this Chapter is to assist the driver to acquire the best possible KNOWLEDGE of the System; he must remember and understand its principles, and this is a matter for mental application.

3. The proper application of the System requires skill, which can only be acquired by practice.

4. The System of Car Control may be defined as:

> A SYSTEM OR DRILL, EACH FEATURE OF WHICH IS TO BE CONSIDERED, IN SEQUENCE, BY THE DRIVER AT THE APPROACH TO ANY HAZARD.

5. A HAZARD is any circumstance, or set of circumstances, which causes the driver to alter course or speed and calls for the whole, or any part, of the System of Car Control to be put into practice. There are three types:

(1) any physical feature such as a cross-road, roundabout, bend or hill-crest;

(2) those created by the movement of other road users; and

(3) those created by variations in road surfaces and weather conditions.

6. The definition requires a driver to CONSIDER EACH FEATURE IN SEQUENCE at the APPROACH to a hazard. These features, which are shown in correct order in the table below, necessitate sound appreciation of the road conditions and correct manipulation of the controls to ensure the safe passage of the vehicle.

Features of the System

Name	Object
(1) COURSE SELECTED. *First* use the mirrors and, if necessary, give the appropriate deviation signal.	To put the car into its correct position for negotiating the hazard, signalling your intention before you do so.
(2) MIRRORS, SIGNALS AND BRAKES. *Before* braking, again use the mirrors and, if necessary, give slow-down and/or deviation signal. (Trafficator.)	To ensure safe speed of approach to, and at, the hazard. To inform other traffic of your intention to deviate.
(3) GEAR, if necessary	To select the correct gear for the speed decided upon at the second feature.
(4) MIRRORS AND SIGNALS. Again use the mirrors and, if necessary, give a deviation signal.	To confirm and, if necessary, emphasise the intention to deviate.
*(5) HORN, if necessary	To warn others of your presence. (They may be within your view but unaware of your presence; or they may be out of your view.)
†(6) NORMAL ACCELERATION AT POINT A.1 OR A.2 IF SAFE. (See FIGURE 1.)	To leave the hazard safely, having regard to road surface and traffic conditions.

Linkages of Controls

7. Drivers already know the following controls, but they should always consider them in *combinations of two*.

---

* Use of the horn in built-up areas at night (11.30 p.m. to 7 a.m.) is prohibited by Regulation.

† This feature applies only to hazards at which the vehicle alters course.

DRIVING MIRROR AND SIGNALS

8. Arm signals, trafficator signals and those made with the horn. Make a habit of this and drivers will find: (a) they will never fail to give a signal if there is following traffic; and (b) signals will be given in plenty of time both to drivers ahead and those behind.

DRIVING MIRROR AND BRAKES

9. This means that when drivers pull up for some obstacle ahead, they will instinctively gauge also the proximity of the nearest vehicle following. Braking systems now incorporate a ' stop ' warning light, but if the following driver is keeping unwisely close, this habit will remind the driver to give a clear slow down signal by hand in plenty of time before braking.

BRAKES AND STEERING

10. Remember that the steering is not improved by braking as you turn a corner. Indeed, if the road is greasy and you brake harshly while turning, there is a risk of a four-wheel skid—the worst sort there is. Brake before the corner at which time the car is travelling in a straight line or nearly so. If by misjudgment you need to brake again, do so with great discretion, otherwise the car will slide bodily.

STEERING AND ACCELERATION

11. This will remind the driver to place the car properly when starting from rest or as he accelerates carefully round a corner. Above all, remember the effect of these two controls when used to make the car skid on the skid pan. Skidding is dealt with in greater detail in Chapter 6.

ACCELERATOR AND GEAR LEVER

12. Drivers should use successively rising gear ratios with firm depression of the accelerator in order to increase speed promptly and lower ratio (or ratios) with a relaxed accelerator in order to help the brakes to reduce speed. The last procedure usually applies to the approach to a corner or an involved traffic situation and enables the driver to be ready to accelerate away from the hazard with the minimum amount of wear and tear to the engine. Use of the gear box is dealt with in more detail in Chapter 6.

GEAR LEVER AND CLUTCH

13. Except for an occasional easing in heavy traffic, the clutch is only to be used for moving off, for gear changing and, in the last few yards, in stopping.

Application of the System

14. With the exception of the combined use of the accelerator, clutch and gear lever during the operation of gear changing, it will be seen that a systematic driver may use different controls in quick succession but need never use two at any one time. His whole plan of driving is mapped out. It is deliberate and thoughtful. Thus, he is master of the machine and is competent to drive it. He should, therefore, be entirely safe on the road.

15. By the correct application of this System the car will at all times be:

    (a) in the right place on the road;

    (b) travelling at the right speed; and

    (c) with the right gear engaged.

16. The application of the System can be illustrated with a diagram depicting any kind of hazard, but a cross-road is used in this case (see Figure 1) because it obviously presents the greatest potential danger. The most difficult manœuvre at a cross-road is the right-hand turn, since an encounter with other traffic coming from any direction is possible. The driver should therefore study Figure 1 (which is not drawn to scale) and imagine he is driving from the bottom of the figure and turning right at the cross-road. The district is a built-up area, so speed of approach will not exceed 30 m.p.h. All six features of the System are shown on the figure and each one is explained in the following paragraphs.

    Note.—As a principle, opposing vehicles turning right at a cross-road should pass offside to offside and turn behind one another but, due to the varying layout of junctions, this must be flexible in its application.

17. *Feature* 1. This is shown with a line commencing at the point marked ' C ' and extending forward and round the corner to the drivers' right. ' C ' stands for ' Course Selected '. The distance of this point from the junction is purely diagrammatic; it cannot be laid down in so many feet or yards as it must vary, mainly according to the speed of approach. The line shows the course to be taken by the driver for this right-hand turn; it is up to, but not over, the crown of the road. Such a course will allow following traffic to overtake on the nearside and also give drivers of approaching traffic an indication, apart from arm signals, of the intention to turn right. In this feature the term ' COURSE SELECTED ' should be understood to mean:

    (a) see and note the position of the road into which you intend to turn;

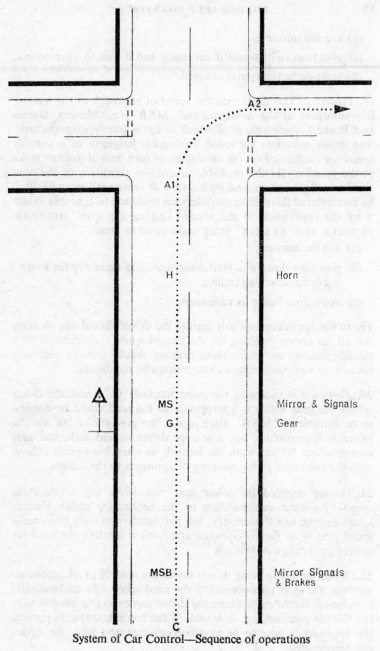

System of Car Control—Sequence of operations

FIGURE 1

(b) use the mirrors;

(c) give turn right signal if necessary and if safe to alter course;

(d) steer on to the course selected.

18. *Feature* 2. This deals with the speed of approach to the hazard. It commences at the point marked 'MSB' (*i.e.*, Mirrors, Signals and Brakes), the position of which is again purely diagrammatic. The driver considers his speed, basing his judgment of a suitable speed for the hazard on (a) the degree of turn he will have to make at the junction, (b) the probable or obvious condition of the road surface at the junction, and (c) his view of other road users likely to be encountered there. If he considers his speed too fast, he will reduce it by the application of this second feature, the term ' MIRRORS, SIGNALS AND BRAKES ' being understood to mean:

(a) use the mirrors;

(b) give slow down and trafficator signals as necessary for following or approaching traffic;

(c) apply foot-brake as necessary.

19. In the application of this feature the driver should aim to carry out all his normal braking for the hazard whilst the vehicle is on a straight course; any subsequent braking should only be necessary because of some unforeseen change in traffic conditions.

20. *Feature* 3 is shown at the point marked ' G ' where the driver selects the gear which is appropriate to the road speed he deemed to be suitable at 'MSB'. Here again, the position of 'G' on the figure is approximate, but a learner driver should make the gear change about 90 feet from the hazard, or when his vehicle is level with the road sign giving warning of approach to the hazard.

21. Having engaged the lower gear, the driver will regulate the speed by correct manipulation of the accelerator pedal. Further speed may be lost if necessary; but it is rarely necessary to increase speed (this is, in fact, a common error, often creating the need for further application of brakes).

22. When the car is being driven under the control of an automatic gearbox, the gear appropriate to the road speed will automatically be selected, but in cases where the driver can expect to have to vary the throttle position, *e.g.* in traffic—if the automatic system permits the appropriate gear to be manually selected and held, the device can be operated.

23. The driver's attention is drawn to the situation as it now stands—the car is in the right position, travelling at the right speed, with the right gear engaged.

24. *Feature* 4 is shown in Figure 1 at 'MS' (*i.e.* Mirrors and Signals). Note the position of this term in relation to ' G '; it follows immediately after. The absence of an interval between the two guards against the common fault of giving late signals. The term 'MS' here means:

  (a) use the mirrors;

  (b) consider again the need for a deviation signal. If the traffic situation has changed it may be necessary to emphasise or confirm the intention to deviate. A signal not previously given may now be required.

25. *Feature* 5 is shown at the point marked ' H '. At this point the driver must consider whether to sound the horn. No hard and fast rule is laid down that it should, or should not, be sounded. The driver should be guided entirely by the circumstances, keeping in mind that use of the horn in no way relieves him of the responsibility of taking every other safety precaution.

26. *Feature* 6. This applies only to hazards which cause the vehicle to pass through a curved path. Note that there are two positions on the curve, 'A.1 ' at the beginning and 'A.2 ' at the end. When the driver gets near enough to the junction he should recognise the condition of the road surface and consider how his tyres will adhere to it. If the surface is good, and if it is safe to proceed, he may apply a normal amount of acceleration from the 'A.1 ' position, so accelerating safely round the curve and out of the hazard.

27. If, however, the road surface is bad for tyre adhesion and, again if it is safe to proceed, he will let the car travel from 'A.1 ' to 'A.2 ' under the influence of the engine just pulling the weight of the vehicle, not increasing the road speed appreciably; and on reaching 'A.2 ', when the rear wheels are again following the front ones in a straight path, the normal amount of acceleration may be applied to increase speed.

28. In his early efforts to apply the System of Car Control, the driver will find that a decided effort of concentration is required to get his brain to work in conjunction with, and as fast as, the speed of the vehicle; therefore, initial practice should be done at quite slow speeds.

B

29. A perfect mind picture of all the six features of the System must be acquired so that, as each feature is considered and dealt with, the next will readily come to mind. Any hesitation or delay caused by wondering which feature comes next will be detrimental to driving technique, because every second of delay represents ground covered by the car. It is wrong to dwell too long on any one feature, otherwise the remaining features cannot have proper consideration.

30. Let us take two examples (Figures 2 and 3) showing how speed of approach and the braking distance can influence the timing of the whole System.

First Example. The driver of a car approaching a cross-road at 60 m.p.h. must see the hazard in good time. It is obvious to him at this stage that he cannot negotiate the cross-road at this speed, and he should assess what speed is suitable. He quickly decides upon the course he intends to follow and applies Feature 2 ('Mirrors, Signals and Brakes') deliberately. Braking, being a hazardous operation at this speed, must be spread over a long distance of road to reduce speed to, say, 20 m.p.h., and so we find that the application of the whole System of Car Control will cover a considerable length of road, owing entirely to the braking distance. (See Figure 2.)

Second Example. The same driver approaches the same cross-road at 40 m.p.h. As before, he must see the hazard in good time, but he can select his course when nearer to it because of his lower speed. For the same reason, he commences to brake at a point nearer to the hazard than if he had been travelling at 60 m.p.h., but he will arrive at a speed of 20 m.p.h. at the same distance from the hazard as in the previous example. (See Figure 3.)

31. It will be seen from Figures 2 and 3 that speed of approach and braking distance must decide the point at which the System is commenced. The result is the same in both cases, for the gear change point is exactly the same and there is time and distance for the remaining features of the System to follow accordingly.

32. Road conditions do not always demand alteration of course, speed or gear; even so, every feature is individually considered. For example, a driver approaches a minor cross-road as he travels at 40 m.p.h. on a main trunk road in flat open country. He observes the cross-road well ahead, and the main road and both converging roads are absolutely clear. He considers his existing course satisfactory. His speed (40 m.p.h.) is quite safe, there is no following traffic and the intention is to go straight on so there is no need to

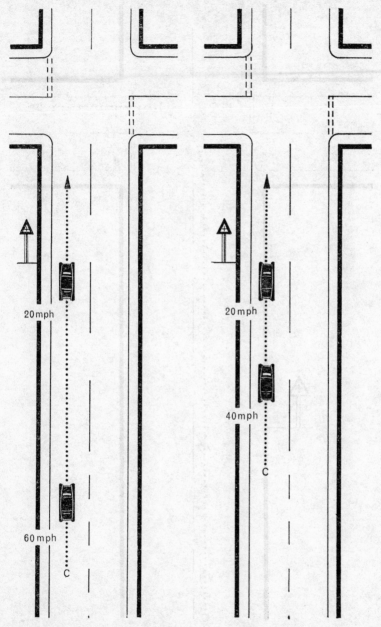

System of Car Control—Achievement the same at different speeds

FIGURE 2   FIGURE 3

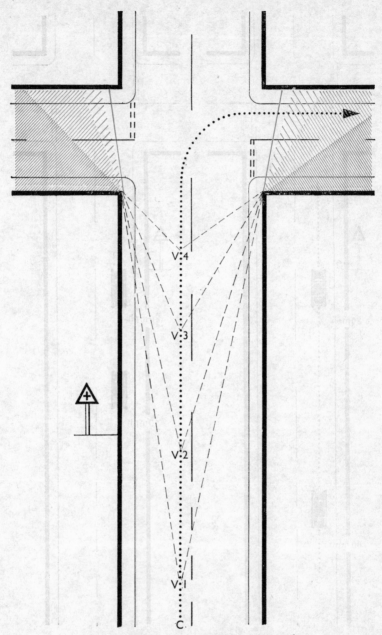

Visibility when approaching a cross-road

FIGURE 4

signal or brake. Still the roads remain quite clear of other traffic and the gear ('top') is quite suitable for the speed and prevailing conditions. He uses the mirrors again but still there is no following traffic and no need for a signal. The converging roads remain quite clear with perfect visibility, and there is thus no need to sound the horn. He passes over the cross-road at 40 m.p.h. with perfect safety. In this example the driver has considered every feature of the System and, being satisfied with the conditions ahead of him at each stage, he makes no change.

33. Road observation by the driver is dealt with in Chapter 4 of this Manual, but it must be mentioned at this point because it is so closely allied to the System of Car Control. Only by perfect observation will the driver become acquainted with the traffic conditions prevailing as he approaches a hazard and when he reaches it. Refer to Figure 4, which shows four points, V.1, 2, 3 and 4, spaced along the road from the beginning of the System up to the hazard. Straight lines drawn from each point to the built-up corners, and then extending across the converging roads, show how the driver's view into the converging roads develops.

34. At V.1, when he selects his course (which is to turn to the right), his view is negligible. From V.1 to V.3 the view improves very little, which shows how necessary it is to approach the hazard with special care. From V.4 to the actual cross-road the view round the corner begins to open up and rapidly improves; and as this is happening the driver should make his decision to increase speed, slow down or stop, according to the position and behaviour of other road users.

35. To negotiate a roundabout the best course to be followed is the shortest distance between the entrance and the exit. When the approach to, and the roundabout, is clear of other traffic this course should normally be adopted. See Figure 5. Where, alternatively, the course could be inconvenient to other traffic, the circumstances demand a different line of approach, manner of negotiating and method of leaving. See Figures 6 and 7.

36. If the intention is to turn left at the roundabout, the course must be to the nearside and the whole approach and system will be applied as for a normal left turn. If the intention is to go straight ahead and other traffic has dictated a course on the nearside, the roundabout should be negotiated on the course shown at Figure 6, *i.e.* leaving enough room for traffic on the offside to circulate with you. Care must be taken not to force this other traffic too far to the offside when leaving; in other words, remain in your own lane. Alternatively, if the line of approach has been in the offside lane, hold this position, leaving enough room for other traffic to enter, circulate and leave on your nearside. If the intention is to turn right at a roundabout, the line of approach should be in the offside lane and the same course followed as in the previous manoeuvre with this difference, that the right turn indicator should be used before entering the roundabout and maintained while keeping to the offside lane in the roundabout. A change to the left turn indicator should be made at the exit before the one by which it is proposed to leave the roundabout.

37. Once the driver has learned to apply the System of Car Control on the approach to each hazard, he should persevere and practise it continually. He will find that it will become almost instinctive and that it is in conformity with Highway Code advice. Furthermore, it will be the foundation upon which the finer points of driving can be built.

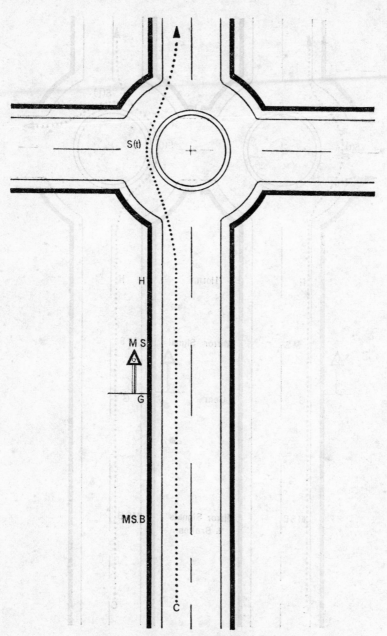

Procedure and signalling at roundabouts

FIGURE 5

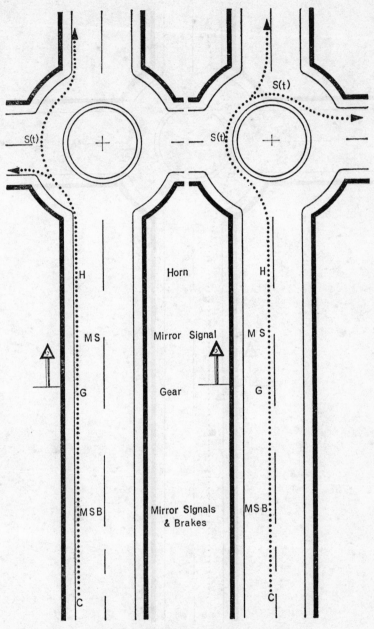

Procedure and signalling at roundabouts

FIGURE 6   FIGURE 7

CHAPTER 3

Drivers' Signals

Object of Chapter

1. Some reference has already been made to the subject of signals in the earlier chapters of this Manual. The object of this chapter is to improve the driver's knowledge of the signals to be given by himself and by other classes of road users.

2. Signs and signals are the language of the road. To ensure the safety of yourself and others, master this language. The Highway Code impresses on drivers the importance of giving correct signals clearly and in GOOD TIME.

3. If every road user, in a spirit of consideration for others, made a consistent effort to perfect his signalling technique as set out in the Highway Code, many accidents would be avoided. Every driver can do a great deal to educate other road users by giving signals which are properly timed and which cannot fail to be understood and appreciated.

4. The 'family tree' below shows how the subject is divided under certain main headings:

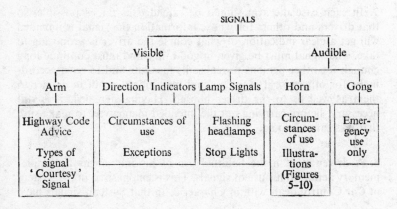

Arm Signals by Drivers

5. General advice as to circumstances demanding the use of signals by car drivers will be found in the Highway Code. Give signals of your intentions correctly, clearly and in good time. [For example, the Code advises the use of the 'Slow Down' or 'Stop' signals when giving way to pedestrians at a zebra-marked crossing. It is an indication not only to drivers behind but also to those approaching the crossing from the opposite direction.]

Drivers' signals as illustrated in the Code are informative. They merely convey notice of an intention to carry out a manoeuvre when indicators or stop lights are not fitted (or are faulty) and also to emphasise or confirm signals previously given. The driver giving the signal must take full responsibility.

6. Three kinds of signal are illustrated:

    (a) ' I intend to move out to the right or turn right'. The palm of the hand faces the front, fingers extended and close together (the arm remaining outside the car for not less than three seconds).

    (b) ' I intend to move in to the left or turn left'. The arm is slowly rotated in an anti-clockwise direction with a flexed elbow, the palm of the hand facing the front.

    (c) ' I intend to slow down or stop'. The palm of the hand, with fingers extended and close together, faces the ground. The arm is slowly lowered and raised several times.

7. In each case the arm should be extended as far as possible, so that drivers and others for whose information the signal is intended will get a clear indication of what course the driver is proposing to take. The signal must be given in good time and must continue long enough for other persons to realise its meaning and to react accordingly, for otherwise it is useless and may indeed result in danger to them as well as to the driver himself. Having signalled, it is still necessary, before carrying out the intended manoeuvre, to make sure that it is safe to do so.

8. A driver must make habitual use of his mirrors as a complementary action to his use of signals. This is emphasised in the System of Car Control dealt with in Chapter 2. In that System, signals have to be considered on three occasions for three distinct changes in running conditions, *i.e.*, ' Course Selected ', ' Mirrors, Signals and Brakes ' and ' Mirrors and Signals '.

9. Let a police officer controlling traffic know clearly by your signal which way you want to go. Signals for this purpose are shown in the Code, the first indicating an intention to go straight on, the second to turn left and the third to turn right, the latter being the orthodox right turn signal. Occasions for using them as information to traffic pointsmen may not be frequent, since correct positioning of a vehicle and normal signals will usually suffice to show a driver's intention. Nevertheless, the arm signals in the Code should be borne in mind and used as necessary.

10. It is appropriate here to include mention of the ' Courtesy Signal ' to be given by a driver as an acknowledgment of a courteous action towards him by another road user. The signal need only be the raising of the left hand towards the forehead; it should not be overdone, nor should it be neglected, for its general use can do much to promote good road manners.

11. Do not rely on signals to go ahead given by unauthorised persons. Statutory power to regulate traffic is vested only in police officers and traffic wardens. Signals by uniformed officials of the motoring organisations should, however, be observed. Don't accept a signal to proceed by any other person without satisfying yourself that it is safe to go on; but a signal to stop should be treated with due respect in the interests of safety as, for instance, when such a signal is given by someone in charge of animals.

12. The expert driver will not only give exemplary arm signals himself, but will also know the signals given by other road users.

Direction Indicators

13. Direction indicator signals are illustrated in the Highway Code and are as follows:

(a) ' I intend to move out to the right or turn right '.

(b) ' I intend to move in to the left or turn left or stop on the left '.

14. Attention is drawn to the correct use of indicator signals when negotiating roundabouts. These are described in paragraphs 35 and 36 of Chapter 2 of this Manual and illustrated in the Highway Code.

15. A common fault is that of leaving indicators in operation long after the turning movement has been completed. This is misleading to others and the Code emphasises that drivers should make sure that the signal is cancelled immediately after use.

Lamp Signals

16. The third form of visible signalling is that of raising or lowering the beam of the headlamps during the hours of darkness. This is an excellent means of giving warning of approach at a road junction or to a driver before overtaking him. To use this form of signalling effectively, the driver must be able to locate the controls without fumbling. The headlamps must be used in good time before reaching the junction or the vehicle to be overtaken. The flashing of head-lamps should not be resorted to as a means of signalling during daylight hours except on motorways, dual carriageways and other fast trunk roads, and then only prior to overtaking when a horn warning would not be heard. (See also Chapter 1, para. 37.) Do not flash excessively or in the face of oncoming traffic, in case dazzle or reflection causes danger to other road users.

17. The stop light fitted at the rear of a vehicle and operating in conjunction with the foot-brake pedal is a useful form of lamp signal, provided vehicles are not travelling so close that it is out of the view of the driver behind. It is not a substitute for the arm signal indicating an intention to slow down or stop. Unlike the arm signal, it does not give immediate indication of the intention to slow down or stop because the light switch is not actuated until some pressure has been applied to the foot-brake pedal, by which time some deceleration has taken place.

18. Before leaving this subject of signals, the driver will be well advised to link together in his mind ' Mirrors and Signals '. Make this a habit and it will ensure that the proximity of following traffic will always be known and that the necessary signals will always be properly given.

Audible Signals

19. The second broad category of signals embraces those which are audible. These are given by sounding the horn and can conveniently be termed ' warning notes '. The gong, bell, siren and two-tone horn, which may only be used on police vehicles, ambulances and fire brigade vehicles, are emergency warning devices and as such are only to be used on occasions of real emergency; even then their use must not be relied on to prevent collisions at cross-roads and similar hazards.

20. The horn should only be sounded when it is really necessary. No hard-and-fast rule can be laid down, but there are certain occasions when the use of the horn is justified, thus:

   (a) to attract the attention of another road user who is obviously vulnerable, despite all other safety precautions taken by the car driver;

   (b) when approaching a hazard where view is extremely poor, or prior to overtaking after every other safety precaution has been taken.

21. In cases under (a) the horn is necessary to draw the attention of road users to impending danger and to get them to co-operate with the car driver to avoid the possibility of an accident (pedestrians, children and cyclists are usually involved).

22. The circumstances in (b) are not quite so obvious; indeed, opinions differ a great deal. What, after all, is the reason for sounding the horn after every safety precaution has been taken? Surely it is to warn of your presence another road user who is not within your view or who, even though visible to you, may be unaware of your approach so that, if he has not already done so, he may take the necessary safety precautions himself.

23. A driver is likely to encounter other road users in these circumstances at every road junction, cross-road, or factory or farm entrance, or whenever he overtakes another vehicle, but it is not suggested that use of the horn is necessary on every such occasion.

24. The driver must realise that experience, intuition, the need for a warning, and the possibility of adopting an alternative driving plan to avoid collision with a thoughtless road user, must be the considerations upon which he must decide to sound, or not to sound, the horn.

25. He will find that, in heavy traffic, occasions for using the horn are rare, primarily because speeds are moderate and other precautions can be taken quickly. In light or medium traffic in built-up areas the need for warning notes will become more frequent, and good judgment coupled with restraint will be necessary to avoid excessive use of the horn. On journeys on unrestricted main roads, where average speeds will be much higher, warning of approach at road junctions will be more readily appreciated. A similar judgment should prevail on minor country roads at the approaches to blind bends, farm entrances, etc.

26. As a general rule, where this is possible, the horn should be operated with the left hand. As a safety precaution when travelling at speed, the hand should not be taken off the steering wheel to operate the horn button or ring, but should slide along a convenient spoke of the wheel, using the thumb to operate the button or ring.

27. Horns should not be sounded in an aggressive or demanding manner, but always courteously, giving plenty of time for other road users to react. For example, the driver who gets very close to a vehicle he is about to overtake at speed and then sounds his horn several times gives the other driver a shock and possibly the impression that the overtaking driver is thrusting and aggressive. Such behaviour is detrimental to the spirit of good fellowship on the road.

28. The horn note should be confined, as far as possible, to one note, either short or long, according to the traffic conditions and the type of road user for whom it is sounded.

29. Figure 8 shows some common occasions for the use of the short note. The driver should imagine he is driving from the bottom of the figure on the course shown, each dot adjacent to the line represents a short horn note given to warn the road user being overtaken and passed.

30. Figure 9 shows two occasions for the use of the long horn note. The driver should imagine he is driving from the bottom of the figure on an unrestricted road at a fairly high speed, and ahead he can see a heavy lorry proceeding steadily on the nearside. Having satisfied himself that it is safe to do so, he will prepare to overtake the lorry and, when about three car lengths from the rear of it, he will give a long note of warning, shown on the figure by a line marked ' Correct '. This note is correct for three reasons: (a) there will be little doubt that it will be heard by the lorry driver, (b) he will have time to react and (c) it will assist him to judge the overtaking vehicle's speed and position. Early and late shorter notes are also illustrated; these are obviously ineffective.

31. Warnings to drivers of vehicles about to be overtaken should not be given automatically, but the following points should be taken into account on such occasions:

(a) Can the overtaken driver be given plenty of room in case he should deviate slightly?

(b) Will unexpected overtaking at speed be likely to disturb him?

(c) Is there any possibility of his deviating without warning, *e.g.*, changing course to enter a garage or other premises?

32. Figure 9 also illustrates the long note sounded at the approach to a minor cross-road when view into the converging roads is obscured by hedges. Assuming that the System of Car Control has been correctly applied, the fifth feature here illustrated must be a long note sounded in good time, since it must carry a considerable distance. It is a good plan to listen for an answering note which, when heard, will call for extra precautions.

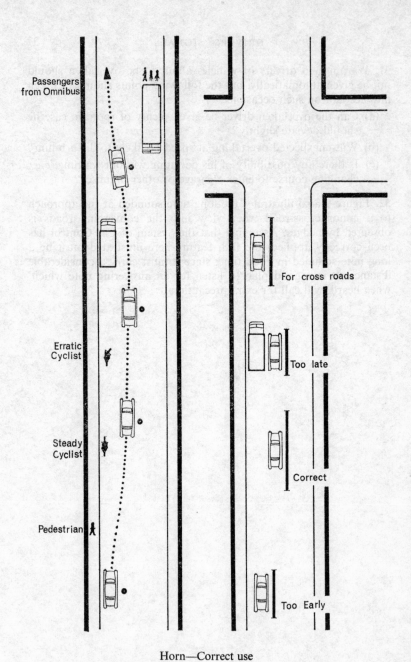

Passengers
from Omnibus

Erratic
Cyclist

Steady
Cyclist

Pedestrian

For cross roads

Too late

Correct

Too Early

Horn—Correct use

FIGURE 8   FIGURE 9

CHAPTER 4

Road Observation

Object of Chapter

1. The object of this chapter is to assist the driver to improve his standard of road observation by considering individual aspects of the subject.

2. The powers of CONCENTRATION and of ROAD OBSERVATION are very closely related, for without the former, success in the latter cannot possibly be achieved. The good driver realises that it is not enough merely to see every detail in a road scene; he must ASSESS THE VALUE of what he sees, and upon that value, formulate his driving plans.

The View from the Vehicle

3. The view a driver obtains from his position at the steering wheel must cover the area to front and sides through an arc of approximately 180 degrees. He must also have the best possible view to the rear through his driving mirrors.

4. The windscreen and all windows must be as clean as possible inside and out; misting of the glass can be prevented by ensuring proper ventilation of the interior of the car. The windscreen washers and wipers must work efficiently immediately they are required. These elementary precautions will do much to prevent the unnecessary handicap of trying to see through glass covered with particles of dust, mud or water.

5. Some obstruction of the driver's view is caused by the coachwork of some saloon cars. In some cases the blind areas to the front can be large enough to mask a pedestrian or pedal cyclist or a road sign. This disadvantage can be most noticeable when side views are required into bends and road junctions. The driver should not make ' heavy going ' of these difficulties; he should merely be conscious of the dangers created and adapt himself to the conditions by moving his head to gain the view he requires in all circumstances. When reversing, the driver's view of a pedestrian to the rear can be obscured

C

by the coachwork of the vehicle, and extra precautions are therefore essential before beginning the reversing movement.

How Vision is affected by Speed

6. Crowds of pedestrians can move about on the pavements of a busy shopping thoroughfare without colliding with one another, not so much because they are all the time looking out for obstructions, but mainly because their speed of movement is so slow that they can change their pace and direction in time to avoid collision. The length and breadth of their view may be short when they move slowly. If, however, one of them wishes to get along quickly he begins to look further ahead, to pick out the places where the crowd is thinnest and to direct his course and increase his speed accordingly. He then finds that his view of other pedestrians at close quarters deteriorates, so that quite often, if one of them comes into his path suddenly, he narrowly avoids collision.

7. The driver of a motor vehicle adjusts the length and breadth of his view in a similar way, but of course, over greater distances, because his speed is a good deal more than that of the pedestrian. When driving at 60 m.p.h. the focal point is a considerable distance ahead and stationary objects there appear clear and well defined, whereas the foreground becomes blurred. At this speed a distinct effort is required to pick out foreground details, and if more than occasional glances are directed at them there will be a natural tendency for the driver to decrease his road speed.

8. When road speed must be kept low owing to traffic conditions, the focal point naturally shortens and the driver observes details. These often indicate that a danger situation is developing and he then has time, owing to his low speed, to take the precautions which will prevent him from becoming involved.

9. From this natural tendency of the eyes to focus according to speed, it is clearly dangerous to drive fast in the wrong places. If traffic is medium to heavy, foreground details must be seen, and to enable the eyes to do this and the brain to function as a result of the stimulus received, speed must be kept within reasonable limits.

10. Fatigue brought about by continuous driving over long periods is first felt as eye strain and lack of concentration, and although special efforts may be made by the driver to maintain his normal standard of observation, he will find the task becomes increasingly difficult, his speed will slacken and his recognition and assessment of danger situations become late and inaccurate.

Weather Conditions

11. Weather conditions such as fog, mist, heavy rain or snow, the fading daylight at dusk and the dazzling brilliance of the setting sun reduce visibility considerably. To meet these conditions speed must be reduced so that objects in the immediate foreground may be seen in time to take evasive action if necessary.

12. When driving in fog switch on headlights and rear lights and, when necessary, the fog lamps. A clearer view may be obtained by the use of windscreen washers and wipers. Proceed at a slow, steady pace and let the nearside kerb or grass verge be your main guide for position. The presence of hazard lines will give warning of approach to a road junction or corner, etc., and at such places these may be valuable landmarks. Be prepared for sudden stoppages of traffic ahead and do not follow too closely. Traffic should only be overtaken when it is really necessary, and then with great care; remember you may lose visual contact with the kerb.

Road Surfaces

13. The average motorist is not so well acquainted with the appearance of road surface types and conditions as he should be. It is useless to complain about a slippery surface after a skid has occurred. The good driver is the one who looks well ahead, recognises any changes of road surface conditions and then applies correct values of braking, acceleration and steering so that maximum road holding is always achieved.

14. When clean and dry, the surfaces of most properly made up roads are good or fairly good for road holding. During inclement weather or when the road is soiled the non-skid value of any surface will deteriorate. Tyres cannot grip a road surface properly if it is wet or soiled by slippery substances such as snow, ice, frost, oil, moist muddy patches or wet leaves, or if it is composed of dry loose dust or gravel.

15. The types of soiling mentioned in para. 14 are all recognisable; they have their own distinctive appearances, which can be seen by the driver as he approaches them. Unfortunately, these conditions are frequently found at the approach to, or at, HAZARDS. The driver already knows that at the approach to HAZARDS running conditions such as steering, braking and acceleration may need alteration, and tyre adhesion to the road surface then becomes of paramount importance.

16. The modern tendency in road construction is for roads to be covered with a non-skid mat which provides a good surface for tyres to bite on. Surface dressings usually consist of stones or chips, or quite fine granules, which are held in position by various tar or bituminous compounds.

17. These surfaces have a dull, coarse, open texture appearance, some, because of the larger chips used, have a more coarse appearance than others. As these surfaces get older they take on a polished appearance owing to wear caused by the passage of traffic. The driver may consider these surfaces as coming in the class known as macadams, the comparative non-skid standard of which is quite high.

18. Concrete road surfaces usually have a distinctive appearance through being light in colour, some have a roughened formation of lateral ribs, most have a good non-skid value. Some, however, are apt to hold surface water which, in cold weather, freezes, creating a slippery surface which is not easily seen.

19. Wood blocks, stone setts and smooth asphalt surfaces are encountered in towns and cities. Their appearance and low non-skid value are well known to the average driver, and great care must be taken when driving on roads of these types to avoid skidding, which will occur from the slightest cause.

20. During wintry weather, road surfaces become frost and ice covered, but not always uniformly; isolated patches and certain gradients remain iced up when other parts have thawed out. The good driver will observe these areas, not only from their appearance but from the behaviour of other vehicles, and will take due precautions in good time to avoid skidding. Remember, tyres travelling on ice make no noise.

21. Wear and tear to the vehicle should be reduced so far as practicable by keeping a good look out for pot-holes, projecting man-hole covers, sunken gullies and any material likely to damage tyres.

To avoid running over such surface conditions alter course slightly if this can be done without detriment to other road users. If they cannot be avoided, speed must be reduced so that rough ground is traversed slowly, thus reducing to a minimum the shock to the vehicle.

Road Signs and Markings

22. The driver's attention is directed to the many types of road signs and markings. It is of the utmost importance that the information or directions they give shall be understood by the driver, and it follows that every sign or road marking must be seen in such good time that the driver will be able to comply with it or profit by the information given.

23. Having seen the sign and understood its meaning, the driver should direct his observation beyond it to the road layout or condition it refers to; he will then have plenty of time to take the necessary action.

24. It is disturbing but true that the average road user does not see and understand the majority of the signs provided for his guidance, unless he makes a special effort or is in search of specific guidance. Every driver should cultivate a special interest in and respect for all signs and markings; by so doing he will improve his road observation and general standard of road behaviour.

Driving Plans

25. A really good driver will formulate his driving plans on the correct assessment of the ever-changing scene ahead and to the rear of his vehicle. He should have a deliberate and calculating temperament, able to make driving decisions without hesitation in a methodical manner at any moment. All decisions must be based on the principle of safety for others as well as himself.

26. He must realise that these driving plans and decisions are made on a combination of:

(a) What he can see.

(b) What he cannot see.

(c) The possible circumstances which may reasonably be expected to develop.

27. Motoring conditions in the British Isles are such that a driver can rarely base his decisions solely on (a) above, because there are many stretches of road where the layout and traffic conditions do not permit an unobstructed view. The greatest difficulties arise from conditions in areas into which the driver cannot see, such as round bends and corners, behind trees and buildings, at places where roads converge or where other traffic obstructs the view of the road beyond.

Zones of Visibility and Invisibility

28. To assist the driver to study the theory of this problem and to improve his driving method, it is possible to divide the road scene into zones or areas, which may be termed zones of visibility and invisibility.

29. Figure 10 illustrates a cross-road in a suburban area. A driver approaching the cross-road from the bottom of the figure and intending to go straight over, will become aware of its presence by seeing the refuge and the hazard warning lines leading up to it; these two outstanding features, if seen in good time, will be sufficient warning of approach to a HAZARD. He will then have time to prepare himself for any eventuality by applying the System of Car Control. The areas coloured red in the converging roads are zones of invisibility, and at the point ' H ' they have receded to a minimum and the zone of visibility is now reaching maximum size. The shaded area may be termed a zone of danger, for it is the intersection of the cross-road where an accident may occur. When the driver gets close to it his position, speed and gear must be such that he is able to take one of two alternatives:

(i) Slow down or stop to allow free passage to other road users.

(ii) Accelerate across and out of the zone of danger if satisfied that no other road user will be endangered or inconvenienced.

30. The size and position of zones of invisibility created by larger vehicles moving ahead are shown in Figures 11 and 12. They show the importance of distance and position in relation to a slow-moving vehicle ahead which, if conditions permit, is to be overtaken. A good view beyond the slow-moving vehicle—both to the near- and off-side of it—is essential before a decision can be made.

31. Figures 11A and 11B show a car 'A' in two positions behind a lorry ' B '. The car in Figure 11A is 90 feet behind the lorry and the car driver can see the nearside kerb up to a point some 100 feet

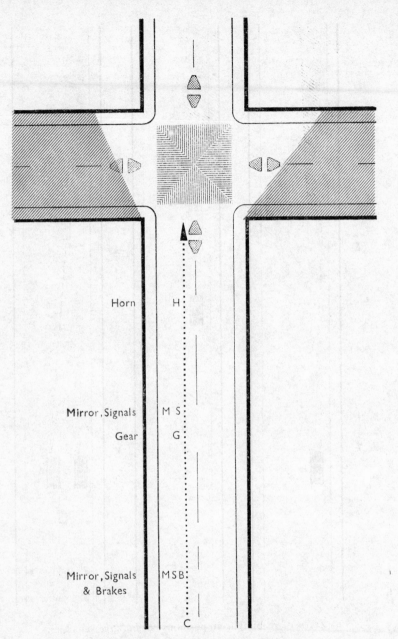

Zone of danger—Suburban cross-road

FIGURE 10

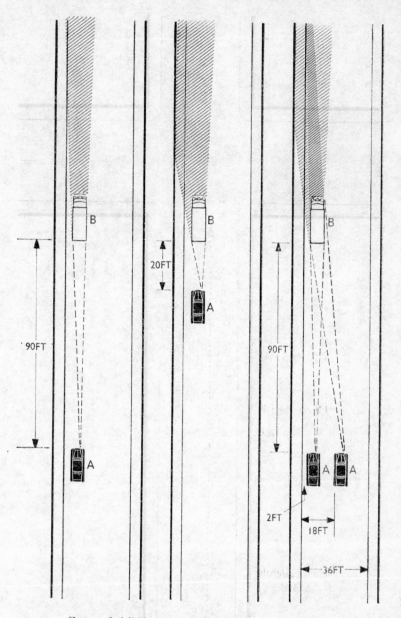

Zones of visibility from positions behind large vehicles

FIGURE 11A   FIGURE 11B   FIGURE 12

beyond the lorry; he also commands a good view along the offside of it. Such a position, therefore, secures a good view and assists the decision to overtake.

32. The car in 11B is positioned 20 feet behind the lorry. The driver loses sight of the nearside kerb just in front of the lorry; he also loses the view of the offside of the road at a point some 170 feet beyond the rear of the lorry.

33. A comparison of the two positions of the car 'A' in Figures 11A and 11B shows that the good driver, before overtaking, will get an early view beyond the lorry when his position in relation to the lorry is most favourable, that is, as in para. 31.

34. Figure 12 shows that position in relation to the width of the road and distance from the back of the lorry can affect the zones of invisibility not only in relation to their size but also in relation to their position. In this figure the car 'A' is shown in two positions. The first position is about 2 feet from the nearside kerb, which gives an unobstructed view of the kerb along the nearside and ahead of the lorry, but an inferior view along the offside. The second position is 18 feet from the nearside kerb, which gives a good view along the offside of the lorry, but a poor view along the nearside.

35. The zone of invisibility in the latter case has not only been kept small by hanging back from the lorry, but has also been moved; in the first position it is almost directly ahead of the lorry, and in the second position it is to the nearside of it. The net result of the two views obtained is almost complete knowledge of the conditions prevailing in front of the lorry, and this is exactly what is wanted for forming a decision to overtake.

36. The observant driver will take full advantage of views across open spaces and through breaks in low positions in hedges, fences or walls, to get that valuable, if brief, view into converging roads which to some drivers appear totally obscured. He will also observe the configuration of the countryside generally and will often be able to judge the severity of any bend or gradient by the position, etc., of trees, hedges or telegraph poles. Figure 13 illustrates the zones of invisibility at the approach to a cross-road. The zone on the driver's right is broken up by gaps in the wall which runs alongside the road. View into the nearside converging road is at first quite poor, but the set-back of the hedge at the actual junction provides a superior

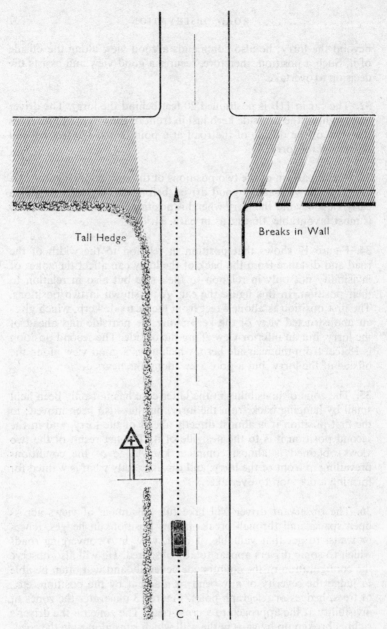

Tall Hedge

Breaks in Wall

C

Zone of visibility at approach to cross-road

FIGURE 13

Road observation—Telegraph poles indicate the severity of a bend

FIGURE 14

view at a later stage to that on the offside, which becomes poor again owing to the presence of the wall.

Figure 14 shows how the telegraph poles give an idea of the severity of the bend in the distance.

37. The length of view a driver obtains at bends and curves on a road which is bordered by hedges, trees or other obstructions can, to a certain extent, be increased or decreased by the position of the car as it approaches such places. Figure 15 shows right- and left-hand bends which are badly obscured by high hedges. A car is shown in alternative positions at the approach to a right-hand bend and in alternative positions at the approach to a left-hand bend. A comparison of the sight lines (marked on the figure) shows that the driver in each case, from position 'A', secures an earlier and longer view round the bend than he does from position ' B '. From this it follows that earlier view into right-hand bends may be obtained by keeping well to the left, and into left-hand bends by keeping slightly over to the right when approaching the bend. Lining up in this way must only be resorted to when it is perfectly safe to do so and, in any case, there must be no encroachment on to the offside of the road.

Road Observation in Town Driving

38. One of the most important aids to successful town driving is local knowledge. To know the situation of main road junctions, one-way streets and roundabout systems, and the type of conditions prevailing there, is undoubtedly of great assistance to a driver because he then has some idea of what to look for.

39. Town driving demands great power of concentration, road observation, the ability to react quickly to changing situations and considerable driving skill. Views ahead are frequently restricted owing to the density of traffic. It is not wise to focus all one's attention on the vehicle immediately in front and a sensible distance should be maintained behind it, so that a view of traffic movement two, three or more vehicles ahead may be obtained from time to time.

40. In places where traffic is really heavy and slow, driving is nothing more than a series of stops and starts. Length of view is short and passage along the road becomes a matter of ' follow my leader '. If, however, there are two or three lines of traffic moving in the same direction, it is important to be in the correct line, especially if a turn to left or right is to be made at the next junction. Appreciation of the advanced directional signs will enable early positioning to be made.

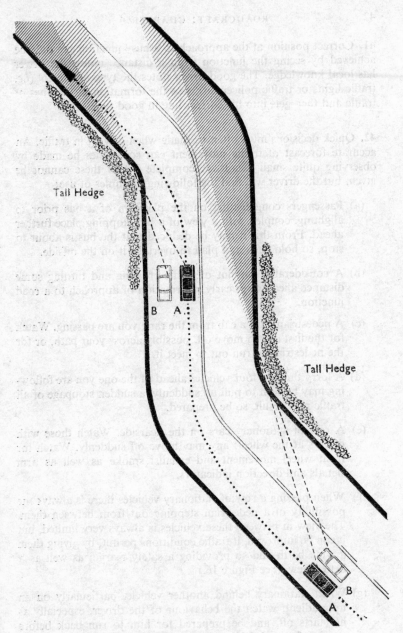

Tall Hedge

Tall Hedge

Positions to give maximum visibility on bends

FIGURE 15

41. Correct position at the approach to a busy junction can only be achieved by seeing the junction from a distance unless the driver has local knowledge. The good driver notes the type of control (*i.e.* traffic lights or traffic policeman), sees the formation of the lines of traffic and then gets into his correct line in good time.

42. Quick decisions must often be made when driving in traffic. An accurate forecast of traffic movement can sometimes be made by observing quite small details. A complete list of these cannot be given, but the driver will find the following examples of use:

(a) Passengers congregating on the platform of a bus prior to alighting, coupled with a view of a bus-stopping place further ahead. From this it may be deduced that the bus is about to stop, so hold back and plan to overtake it on the offside.

(b) A considerable amount of traffic crossing and turning some distance ahead gives early information of approach to a road junction.

(c) A pedestrian hails a cab from the rank you are passing. Watch for the first cab to move off, possibly across your path, or for the pedestrian to run out to meet it.

(d) A lorry three or four vehicles ahead of the one you are following may be seen to pull up suddenly, a sudden stoppage of all traffic may result, so be prepared.

(e) A row of stationary cars on the nearside. Watch those with drivers at the wheel; any may move off suddenly. Watch for front wheel movement and exhaust smoke as well as arm signals and direction indicators.

(f) When passing a row of stationary vehicles there is always the possibility of a pedestrian stepping out from between them. The view in between these vehicles is always very limited, but it can be improved, if traffic conditions permit, by giving them a wide berth and so providing a safety margin as well as a better view. (See Figure 16.)

(g) When stationary behind another vehicle, particularly on an up-gradient, watch the behaviour of the driver, especially as he starts off, and be prepared for him to run back before moving forward. Make allowance for this by not drawing up too close.

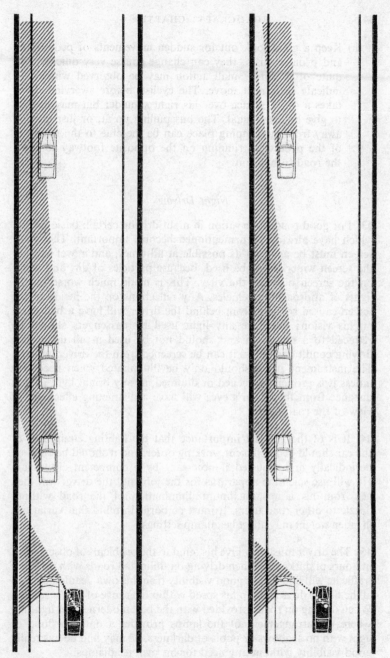

Blind areas beyond parked cars—position to give maximum visibility

FIGURE 16

(h) Keep a good look out for sudden movements of pedestrians and pedal cyclists; they can change course very quickly, but quite often some small action may be observed which will indicate their next move. The cyclist, before swerving right, takes a quick glance over his right shoulder but may neglect to give an arm signal. The bus pulling up at, or just moving away from, a stopping place can be the clue to the intention of the pedestrian running on the opposite footway to cross the road to board it.

Night Driving

43. For good road observation in night driving certain basic factors which have already been mentioned become important. The windscreen must be as clean as possible at all times, and in wet weather the screen wipers must be used, because particles of dirt and water on the screen obstruct the view. This is made much worse by the lights of approaching vehicles. Any reflections on the inside of the screen caused by light from behind the driver will have a bad effect on his vision; therefore any light used by passengers should be reduced to a minimum and should not be used at all under fast driving conditions unless it can be screened from the driver entirely. The instrument panel should only be illuminated when necessary unless it is properly screened or dimmed, as any bright light at that distance from the driver's eyes will have a distracting effect on his view of the road ahead.

44. It is of the greatest importance that the lighting equipment of the car should be in efficient working order, and it should be checked periodically and adjusted if necessary by a competent electrician. He will use scientific apparatus for the job, and the driver will then get from his lamps maximum illumination of the road without dazzle to other road users. It must be borne in mind that variations in laden weight may affect headlamp settings.

45. The driver must now give his mind to the problems of observation in hours of darkness. When driving on unlighted roads with no other traffic he will find he has good visibility from his own headlamps, and all he has to do is to keep his speed within the range of that visibility. When driving on roads provided with the best modern street lighting, where the arrangement of the lamps provides a uniform flood of light with no shadows or pools of darkness, he may find he has really good visibility without any need for his own headlamps.

46. The favourable conditions mentioned in the previous paragraph are quite rare, however, and more usually the night driver finds he is at times harassed by the glare or dazzle of approaching vehicle headlamps and the frequent pools of darkness or shadow caused by inferior street lighting.

Dazzle

47. Not infrequently a driver will be dazzled by a glare of lights from an approaching vehicle, particularly if its headlamps, though dipped, are badly adjusted. The greatest difficulty is experienced immediately after the glaring lights have passed because the eyes take a little time to adjust themselves to the sudden reduction of light which follows. On such occasions the driver is advised to keep his temper and to control his natural impulse to retaliate by switching his headlights full on. He should avoid looking straight at the approaching headlamps and should direct his eyes to the nearside of the road ahead, keeping a particular lookout for pedestrians and vehicles; he will then get some benefit from the illumination of the road by the approaching lights. He should slow down or stop, and as soon as the offending driver has passed he may switch on full headlamps to overcome the ensuing blackness. Finally, the driver should bear in mind that this evil of dazzle, whilst bad at times, is by no means continuous. He will find that, if he makes a practice of using his own anti-dazzle device as he approaches oncoming traffic, the same courtesy will, as a rule, be extended to him.

48. One of the most difficult problems which besets the night driver is found in built-up areas where the street lighting is inferior. Frequently he finds that his view consists alternatively of pools of light from street lamps and of darkness where the street lighting fails to penetrate owing to lack of power or to obstruction by over-hanging trees. He is advised to illuminate these pools of darkness by using his headlamps whenever he can do so without danger to other road users. Frequently, of course, this will be impossible owing to approaching traffic, and in this event he should drive on his dipped headlamps at a speed suited to the conditions. It is dangerous to black out completely by driving on sidelamps only.

49. The driver will find that, whilst his own lights illuminate many objects on the road, he will see a great deal from the lights of other vehicles, particularly those approaching. The glare of the headlights of traffic approaching round bends or coming along converging roads gives ample warning of approach and also a guide to the severity of bends and corners. Objects on the road ahead often appear as silhouettes in the approaching lights.

50. Night driving is always a severe test of endurance. A driver should prepare himself by taking sufficient rest beforehand. Fatigue will first be felt as eye strain, for continuous looking along a beam of light is most tiring. If drowsiness overtakes him he should not try to overcome it whilst still driving; he should stop, ' have a stretch ', rest his eyes for a little while and have a drink of hot tea or coffee. Any change from driving will restore the failing power of concentration and observation.

CHAPTER 5

Acceleration, Braking and Steering

Object of Chapter

1. This chapter opens a field of study in greater detail for the more advanced driver. Much of the material has been dealt with in a broad sense in the earlier chapters of this Manual, but it is hoped that the driver will realise that it is attention to the finer points of driving that will fit him to be classed as an expert.

2. The moment a driver puts a motor vehicle into motion he accepts a great responsibility. He can cause the vehicle, a mass weighing a ton or more, to move forward or backward at varying speeds, turn to either side sharply or gradually, and stop suddenly or smoothly, just when he wishes, provided he manipulates the controls accurately (in this his physical and mental condition will play no small part—see Chapter 1).

3. The System of Car Control, with which the driver should now be familiar, was explained in Chapter 2, but of necessity in such a broad manner that no attention was given to the details of acceleration, braking and steering. These details and the manner in which they affect the car will be discussed in the following paragraphs.

Acceleration

4. Let the driver first get a clear impression in his mind of what is meant by 'Acceleration' as applied to driving a motor vehicle. It is the increase in road speed of a moving car brought about by the control exercised by the driver with his right foot and the accelerator pedal. (We are not here considering acceleration developed by a car in such unusual circumstances as running away and coasting down a hill with increasing speed because the brakes have failed.)

5. The acceleration capabilities of different cars vary considerably according to the efficiency of the engine and power weight ratio. A high maximum speed on any given journey is not very useful if it takes a considerable time and lengthy stretch of suitable road to attain it.

6. High average speeds under ordinary road conditions are usually achieved by the modern car not because of its high maximum road speed, but more by its excellent power to accelerate, when suitable gears are used, from quite slow speeds.

7. How is acceleration produced? As the pressure of the driver's foot depresses the accelerator pedal it enlarges the carburettor throttle valve opening and an increased amount of combustible mixture is admitted to the cylinders of the engine. This increase of mixture will produce, if the power available is equal to the driving conditions, an increase of revolutions per minute of the engine which will be transmitted to the driving wheels and the car will accelerate.

8. The accelerator pedal is spring-loaded to its closed position and the driver must acquire the ' feel ' of this spring loading in order to open the throttle valve at all times smoothly. The accelerator pedal and linkage, right through to the carburettor, must be in perfect working order; it will be extremely difficult to control speed with the accuracy which is necessary if this linkage is fouled by floor-boards or mats or has any slackness to be taken up by the initial movement of the pedal.

9. To describe the length of movement of the accelerator pedal in various circumstances will not be of much assistance to the driver, but an attempt to describe how that movement is to be effected may be helpful.

10. First, he is advised to wear light footwear, preferably shoes; this is really important because the sensation of pedal movement and accurate ' feel ' of the operation of foot pedals cannot effectively be transmitted to the brain through thick-soled heavy boots or shoes.

11. The right foot operates the accelerator and foot-brake pedals, but for most of the time it is on the accelerator pedal. Therefore the right heel should rest on the floorboard approximately midway between, and to the rear of, these two pedals; it will support the weight of the right leg. The ball of the foot should fall naturally forward and downward on the accelerator pedal. The ankle must be flexible to allow the foot to rise or fall at will from the pivot created by the heel. At this stage the driver should understand that although the heel acts as a pivot for accelerator pedal movement, it will not serve the same purpose when pressure is applied on the foot-brake pedal.

12. An engine will only respond to an increase of pressure on the accelerator pedal if it can develop the power to do the work demanded of it. All references now made to acceleration will be on the assumption that the correct gear is engaged and that road and running conditions are such that an increase of road speed is desirable and possible with safety.

13. Effective acceleration is only possible when a useful and, it may be stressed, economical increase of the engine revolutions per minute is obtainable, and to this end the use of the gearbox must be considered. For instance, a driver wishing to get high speed as quickly as possible from a car fitted with a four-speed gearbox would be unwise to use more than 50 per cent of maximum r.p.m. in second gear, or more than 75 per cent of maximum r.p.m. in third gear. Any rate of r.p.m. above these approximate figures for the average car would be unproductive of the acceleration wanted, and uneconomical in fuel consumption. For normal driving the percentages above are on the high side.

14. Generally, when the accelerator pedal is depressed with a rough, sudden, jerky movement, the car will jump forward, suddenly increasing road speed, but if the pedal is depressed steadily and progressively, the same increase of road speed will be obtained but without the sudden jump and jerk. Obviously the latter manner of depression will cause less wear and tear and will produce smoothness of movement. On a car fitted with automatic transmission, acceleration through the gears is automatically controlled, but faster acceleration is obtained by depressing the accelerator pedal to give a large throttle opening, when gear changing up is delayed to a pre-set maximum engine speed. A rapid burst of acceleration by means of a lower gear can be obtained by depressing the accelerator pedal fully (' kick-down '), when the next lower gear is automatically engaged within the pre-set limits of engine speed.

The Behaviour of a Car under the Influence of Acceleration

15. Acceleration has a considerable effect upon the behaviour of a car as it proceeds along the road. Figure 17 shows that, when under the influence of acceleration, a car tends to settle down on to the road, particularly at the rear end, tending to improve the grip of the tyres on the road surface, thus achieving a condition of maximum stability.

Acceleration—weight thrown rearward
FIGURE 17

16. This favourable behaviour of the car under acceleration is more forcibly realised when it is compared with the behaviour of a car under the influence of braking (see para. 34 below). The driver should also realise that this condition of good stability prevails not only under acceleration, but also when the weight of the vehicle is being propelled by a pulling engine with no increase of road speed.

Acceleration Sense

17. Acceleration sense may be defined as the ability to vary the speed of the car according to the existing road and traffic conditions when braking is not demanded. It is a skill found only in really good drivers, but is latent in many and may be developed by improved judgment of speed and distance, and practice. A driver who possesses acceleration sense recognises the speed both of the vehicles he is following and of those which are approaching. He also takes into account any variation of speed that may occur owing to changing conditions which develop ahead. He decides upon a safe distance to keep between his vehicle and the one in front by acceleration, deceleration or constant road speed. In the light of these considerations he will adjust his speed by suitable variations of pressure on the accelerator pedal, avoiding braking unless it is absolutely necessary, so that he keeps progressive station in the general flow of traffic. He may overtake certain slow-moving vehicles with a suitable degree of acceleration when it is safe to do so, and will at the same time be prepared to reduce his speed by timely deceleration if an inconsiderate driver overtakes and then cuts in.

18. The distance a driver decides to maintain between the front of his vehicle and the rear of the one ahead, when there is no intention to overtake, is dependent upon the speed of both vehicles, the condition of the road surface, his reaction and his driving ability.

As a guide to this distance it is suggested that at speeds up to 30 m.p.h. not less than one foot per mile an hour is suitable. At speeds over 30 m.p.h. the distance should of course be increased, and not less than one yard per mile an hour should be allowed.

19. Acceleration sense is one of the important skills which, allied to others, makes overtaking on fast roads a well timed, brisk and safe manœuvre. Figures 18, 19 and 20 illustrate a skilful driver's judgment and use of acceleration as he leads up to the act of overtaking a slow moving vehicle on a fast road.

20. In Figure 18 the driver of car 'A' is travelling quite fast towards a lorry 'B', which he plans to overtake. The situation is complicated for him by the presence of the approaching cars 'C' and 'D'. He recognises the situation in good time and, from their speed and distance, realises that the cars 'C' and 'D' have the right of way and that he must not be sandwiched between two lines of moving vehicles. He therefore eases his speed by early deceleration.

21. Figure 19 shows the relative positions of the vehicles a fraction of a second later. The important vehicles are now the lorry 'B' and the car 'D', which are now opposite one another. The driver of car 'A' now accelerates, not fiercely but steadily, to close up the gap between himself and 'B'.

22. Figure 20 shows the final phase when the driver of car 'A' is accelerating firmly along the offside of the lorry 'B'.

23. The technique of the experienced driver who drives fast but considerately is well worth close study, and it will be found that he makes full use of the power of acceleration of his car at every opportunity in a safe yet deliberate manner.

24. First of all he knows the capabilities of his car; he will not drive fast until he is familiar with its behaviour and he will never demand more of it than he knows he can get.

25. The changing conditions of the road surface will never escape his attention, and he will drive his car in such a way that he makes full use of acceleration where the surface is in good condition and eases his speed in the bad places.

26. His approach to bends and corners will be perfect demonstrations of every feature of the System of Car Control, and his technique of

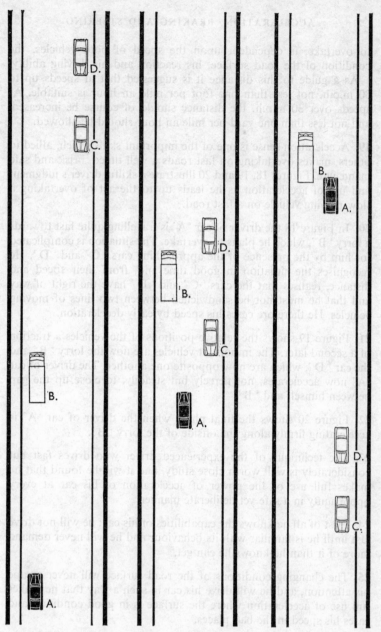

Acceleration sense applied to overtaking

FIGURE 18   FIGURE 19   FIGURE 20

acceleration will reveal a perfect timing of the application of the correct degree of acceleration as his car commences, traverses and leaves its curved path. The car will enter the curve at a safe speed, the engine pulling the load, and as the view of the road out of the hazard opens up and the steering is straightened, he increases acceleration. So the car has entered the hazard at a slow or moderate speed according to the severity of the bend, and has left it by firm and safe acceleration. The driver's continued aim has been to maintain tyre adhesion to the road surface under the adverse conditions of a bend, coupled with brisk movement of the car by a careful balance of acceleration and steering.

27. Finally, the driver will realise that acceleration properly used can be a contributing factor to his safety in certain hazardous or dangerous situations. For it is possible to accelerate out of danger, as well as to brake. Braking sometimes results in stopping right in the path of approaching danger.

28. Drivers of cars fitted with certain types of automatic transmission should remember that there may be little braking power from the engine when pressure on the accelerator pedal is released. This will have an effect on the extent to which acceleration sense can be employed. Whenever conditions indicate that frequent variations of throttle position will occur and a lower gear would normally have been engaged, use can be made of any device that is fitted to enable the lower gear to be engaged with full braking effect from the engine. In the following paragraphs on 'Braking' the importance of this characteristic of cars fitted with automatic transmission will be understood and must be considered when these paragraphs are being studied and their teaching applied.

Braking

29. There are two normal methods by which the speed of motor vehicles may be reduced: (a) by the deceleration of the engine as the pressure on the accelerator pedal is relaxed, and (b) by the application of the brakes.

30. It will be appreciated that the previous discussion on acceleration did, to some extent, deal with the loss of road speed brought about by normal deceleration. When pressure on the accelerator pedal is relaxed the engine will slow down due to the compression in the cylinders, and this slowing down will be transmitted to the driving wheels. Thus the engine is acting as a brake on the speed of the car.

Braking—weight thrown forward

FIGURE 21

31. This method of reducing speed will be smooth and gradual; it will have little detrimental effect on the grip of the tyres on the road, and unnecessary wear and heating of the brakes will be avoided. The loss of road speed by engine deceleration will be more pronounced when a low gear is engaged. This will be valuable when driving on slippery roads where normal braking would be likely to lock the road wheels and cause skidding, or when making long descents in hilly country, when heavy continuous brake application would cause overheating of the brake shoes and drums. In these circumstances use can be made of any device fitted to cars with automatic transmission, permitting the engagement and holding of a lower gear with full engine braking.

32. Generally, however, deceleration by using the engine is a lengthy process, and although effective use is made of it in the initial stage of every reduction of road speed, the ordinary road wheel brakes must be brought into action quite frequently.

33. The elimination of unwanted road speed by the application of road wheel brakes can be one of the most difficult and hazardous controlling operations carried out by a driver. This is especially so when the brakes are applied at speed.

34. Braking is hazardous because of the effect it has on the car. Figure 21 shows, to an exaggerated extent, the behaviour of a moving car under the influence of braking. The rear tends to lift, weight is thrown forward and downward on to the front wheels, and the resulting unequal distribution of weight makes the steering heavier and reduces the general stability of the car, especially at the rear wheels.

35. The driver will readily observe that the conditions prevailing when the car is under the influence of braking are a complete reversal of the favourable conditions found when the car was under the influence of acceleration.

36. In order to reduce as far as possible the difficulties and disadvantages previously described, the driver must learn to apply intelligently the following three rules for all normal braking:

(1) Brake only when travelling straight, that is, not in a bend or when skidding. This means you must brake in plenty of time for whatever hazard you are approaching.

(2) Let your brake pressure vary with the condition of the road surface. Choose a coarse, firm and dry section of road for firm braking, and ease off the pedal pressure for a loose or slippery road surface. This calls for continued observation of road surface conditions.

(3) When descending a steep winding hill, maintain firm braking on the straight stretches, and brake as lightly as possible in bends or corners. Remember the value of engaging a lower gear at an early stage in the descent.

37. When braking, every effort should be made to reduce speed as safely and smoothly as possible, thereby minimising the wear and tear to the car generally and the generation of heat at the brake drums or discs.

38. The foot-brake pedal is operated with the ball of the right foot, and the heel cannot act as a pivot for the foot in the same way as it did when controlling the accelerator pedal.

39. The initial effort required to move the brake pedal will be greater than that required to move the accelerator. However, with the modern trend towards servo assistance, the pressure required is less than that needed to operate a manual system. The first part of the pedal movement will merely take up the free movement of the braking system. Then the brake shoes or pads will make contact with the brake drums or discs, which are revolving with the road wheels. Normally, this contact should be made as lightly as possible, and once established it should be made harder, as necessary, by increased pressure on the pedal. Servo assistance does not alter braking efficiency but makes the application easier.

40. The pressure on the brake pedal should be eased off gradually as the unwanted road speed is lost, so that as the car comes to rest it glides to a stop on an even keel, entirely without jerk or settling down suddenly at the rear end.

41. Progressive brake application is superior to sudden hard application; all late heavy braking should be confined to the rare occasions when an emergency stop is needed. The good driver should estimate the distance he requires to stop, or slow down appreciably, from all road speeds, and he will commence his braking in time to reduce speed with safety and smoothness. Again, the driver is advised to judge the effect of his effort on the brake pedal by the variation in the speed of the vehicle.

The Brake Test under Running Conditions

42. The driver's attention is drawn to the necessity for checking the operation of the hand- and foot-brake controls on first entering the car.

43. Assuming these tests prove satisfactory, the driver should, as soon as possible after getting the car moving on the road, test the brakes under running conditions. This test is to show him the manner in which the vehicle responds to normal braking; it is a test of firm progressive braking, but not a crash stop to lock the road wheels.

44. The method of testing is as follows. If possible, choose a level stretch of road with a good surface; then, whilst travelling at 30 m.p.h. in top gear, apply the brakes with medium initial firmness and then progressively harder, so that the vehicle loses road speed rapidly without locking any road wheels. During the test, due regard must be given to the safety and convenience of other road users.

45. The result of the test should show that the vehicle can be pulled up on a straight course without swerving or lurching to either side. There should be no tendency for any wheel to lock; the best braking is obtained when the wheels are just revolving.

46. The information given in the foregoing paragraphs on reducing road speed may be consolidated in the driver's mind by the following example. Imagine driving at speed along a fast main road with a good view ahead, and approaching a road junction where a 90 degree left-hand turn will be made.

(a) The driver must OBSERVE the following features as early as possible:

(1) The road junction layout, which is a hazard.

(2) The condition of the road surface as it opens up ahead.

(3) The other traffic ahead and to the rear; and possible changes in traffic conditions during the approach.

(b) The driver must DECIDE:

(1) To select the best course, bearing in mind that he will be braking very firmly.

(2) The approximate speed at which he will turn the corner.

(3) Where he will commence braking to bring his existing speed down to that which he estimated would be suitable for turning the corner.

(c) The driver will comply with the following requirements in his MANIPULATION OF CONTROLS:

(1) The car must be travelling as straight as possible during braking.

(2) The initial brake application will be as light as possible.

(3) Brake pressure will then be increased as necessary.

(4) During the period of firm braking considerable heat may be generated at the brake drums, and it will be beneficial from time to time to relax the pedal pressure momentarily, re-applying it delicately. This method will be profitable especially if the road tends to be slippery. (In this connection it should be borne in mind that, if the car has been driven through pools of water, the operation of the brakes may have been impaired through water seeping on to them.)

(5) The speed will be reduced to that decided at (b) (2), when braking will cease in time for the remaining features of the System of Car Control to be considered before the turn is made.

This example is similar to but more detailed in the matter of braking than those given in Chapter 2, para. 18, where the System of Car Control was discussed.

Steering

47. One of the main requirements in the proper control of a motor car is to ensure that it is always in the right place on the road, whatever the circumstances. Obviously this is done by the driver's ability to steer accurately and safely. In order that he may do this, the steering and suspension must be in good condition and, in addition, the tyre treads and air pressures must be correct.

48. The driver should realise that different makes of cars have steering characteristics which are peculiar to themselves. Hence, drivers are heard to remark that a car's steering is heavy or light, or that it is high- or low-geared. In any case these characteristics have their advantages and disadvantages in certain circumstances, and it is the driver's duty to recognise them and adapt himself accordingly; this particularly applies to cars fitted with power steering.

49. Power steering is a method of giving assistance to the driver by hydraulic pressure from an engine-driven pump. Therefore, no assistance is available unless the engine is running, but when it is, the driver can, by exerting pressure on the steering wheel of between 5 lbs. and 10 lbs., turn the wheel from lock to lock with extreme ease, even when stationary. This last practice causes undue stress and strain on tyres, steering, linkage and suspension and is deprecated. A light movement by the driver is accentuated by the hydraulic assistance, and care must be taken to prevent the application of too much steering or over correction, as there is a slight loss of ' feel ' by the driver.

50. Good road observation is necessary so that the driver may see road traffic conditions all round the vehicle; then he may place his car in the best position available to him, subject to the advice in the Highway Code and this Manual.

51. A modern car in good order will keep to a straight course on a straight and level road with little or no steering control by the driver. Since, however, modern roads are not level but have a camber, a car being driven on the nearside of the road tends to run down the camber towards the nearside, or towards the offside if being driven on the offside of the road. This tendency can be overcome easily by the minimum of steering control.

52. The driver will find that a motor vehicle moving on a straight course will be travelling under the most favourable conditions so far as directional control is concerned. As soon as it is moved into a curved path, the stability of the vehicle deteriorates and control becomes more difficult. The driver should therefore aim to make all deviations from the straight course as gradually and smoothly as possible, avoiding any steering movement of a sudden or jerky nature which will be detrimental to the grip of the tyres on the road.

53. Steering success or failure originates in the driver's deportment in the driving seat. He should be seated in an upright position; not taut or strained, yet not too relaxed or seated primarily for comfort. The seating position advised will be found advantageous when the car is skidding or cornering, for in these circumstances the body is apt to roll with the alteration of weight distribution and the steering wheel may be moved unintentionally. Some additional support may be obtained by bracing the left leg from a firm position taken with the left foot on the floorboards.

54. The normal basic position of the hands on the wheel on a straight road should approximate to the hands on a clock at the time of ten minutes to two. It will enable him to effect any emergency movement of the wheel which may be demanded, and his arms and elbows will have freedom for all necessary arm movements.

55. Movements of the arms to control the steering wheel will originate where the upper arm joins the shoulder, the wrists and elbow joints acting as shock absorbers. The grip of the hands on the wheel rim should normally be light, with a readiness at all times to tighten if necessary. A tight grip continuously maintained can make for rough movements of the wheel, which are seldom necessary. The fingers should fold round the rim in a natural manner; such mannerisms as the palm of the hand holding the wheel with fingers outstretched or the fidgeting of the hands on the wheel should be avoided. Remember also that the wheel is provided for the driver to steer with and not as a support for his arms. The driver is advised that the movement of his hands often reflect his state of mind, they can indicate his confidence, or lack of it, to the critic.

56. On the average private car all normal deviations from the straight course can be made by following the under-mentioned guiding principles:

(1) The hand on that side of the wheel corresponding to the turn to be made should pull down on the wheel from a high position.

(2) The other hand should allow the wheel rim to slide through it or, if the turn is severe, it may drop to a low position ready to push upwards if necessary.

57. Such hand and arm movements alternately pulling down and pushing up may have to be repeated if the turn to be made is of a sharp ' hairpin ' nature or if the car has particularly low-geared steering.

58. Having turned the car sufficiently, it must be straightened again or it will continue in a circular path. Accordingly, the steering wheel should be fed back by hand movements similar to those in para. 56, but in the reverse direction. The steering on most cars has an automatic self-straightening action; on some, this may be quite powerful and restraint will have to be exercised on the wheel to prevent the car straightening up too soon.

59. By the methods in paras. 56–58 steering into a turn and out again will be accomplished either slowly or quickly according to the road speed but in any case smoothly and progressively.

60. The driver should note, from the description of the position of the hands and their movements on the steering wheel, that each hand keeps to its own side of the wheel. Never, when the car is being driven forward, should either hand pass the 12 o'clock position.

STEERING WHEN REVERSING

61. When reversing, the driver must turn his head to look over his right or left shoulder, and the basic hand-hold on the wheel must be at the top of the wheel near the 12 o'clock position. When he looks over his right shoulder his left hand should take this position, and when he looks over his left shoulder his right hand should be so placed. The steering wheel may then be turned either to left or right. During this procedure the free hand may adopt a low position approximating to four or eight o'clock as the case may be, either with a loose hold allowing the wheel to slide through it, or to hold the wheel in position whilst a new grip is taken at the top.

Five Rules for Steering and Steering Faults

62. (1) Your right elbow must not rest on the top of the offside door or window frame. This attitude restricts the use of the arm.

(2) Your hands must be placed on the wheel so that you are able to exert maximum leverage, if necessary.

(3) On a straight road your hands should settle in the effective position (ten to two), not gripping tightly but being ready to do so.

(4) Normally you should tighten the grip when cornering and braking, both hands holding the wheel during these operations.

(5) Do not tighten the grip when on a greasy or slippery road; it may tend to roughen your movements of the wheel, so inducing skidding.

63. The following common steering faults should be avoided:

(a) Allowing the hands to drop down to a position in the lower half of the steering wheel.

(b) Allowing the hands to fidget or move unnecessarily on the wheel.

(c) Removing either hand from the wheel for unnecessarily long periods when gear changing.

(d) Removing both hands from the wheel.

(e) Gripping the wheel too tightly.

(f) Turning in a given direction too much or maintaining a given turn for too long. This often results, especially with a novice driver, in the car describing a ' weaving ', erratic course.

(g) Trying to fix the position of the car on the road by continuously sighting one point on the car with a special feature in the road layout. NOTE: This is a useful procedure when moving the car very slowly in a confined space, *e.g.*, in a garage.

(h) Making sharp deviations out of, or into, a straight course (*i.e.*, cutting out or cutting in when overtaking stationary or slow-moving vehicles or other obstructions).

(i) Failing to allow sufficient safety margin on the nearside when overtaking other vehicles or obstructions. NOTE: Six feet of clearance has been found to be a good margin of safety if such space is available. This distance is given only as a guide, as frequently a driver will have to decide on a suitable margin of safety in the light of prevailing conditions.

64. The driver should bear in mind that other driving faults will produce conditions which will make steering difficult. The most important of these are:

(a) Poor road observation.

(b) Entering bends and corners too fast.

(c) Braking in bends and corners.

E

65. The importance of a driver's ability to concentrate and react quickly to emergencies and changing road conditions cannot be overstressed, especially with regard to steering. One of the evasive actions often demanded to avoid an accident situation is an alteration of direction at short notice.

66. The main features of this section are illustrated in Figure 22, which shows a sharp bend, normally cambered; there is no obstruction of view or other traffic, but the road surface conditions present the greatest difficulty because they are wet, dry, greasy and dry again. The figure is self-explanatory, and the driver should note the course as the car approaches and leaves the bend, and the braking and acceleration values on the different conditions of road surface.

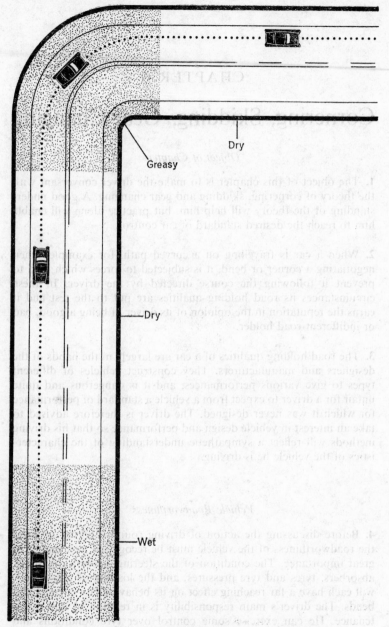

Braking—attention to quickly varying road surfaces

FIGURE 22

CHAPTER 6

Cornering, Skidding, Gear Changing

Object of Chapter

1. The object of this chapter is to make the driver conversant with the theory of cornering, skidding and gear changing. A good understanding of the theory will help him, but practice alone will enable him to reach the desired standard of car control.

2. When a car is travelling on a curved path, for example, when negotiating a corner or bend, it is subjected to forces which tend to prevent it following the course directed by the driver. In these circumstances its road holding qualities are put to the test and it earns the reputation in the opinion of its driver of being a good, bad or indifferent road holder.

3. The road holding qualities of a car are largely in the hands of the designers and manufacturers. They construct vehicles of different types to give various performances, and it is dangerous and quite unfair for a driver to expect from a vehicle a standard of performance for which it was never designed. The driver is therefore advised to take an interest in vehicle design and performance so that his driving methods will reflect a sympathetic understanding of the characteristics of the vehicle he is driving.

Vehicle Roadworthiness

4. Before discussing the action of driving round a corner or bend the roadworthiness of the vehicle must be recognised as a matter of great importance. The condition of the steering, suspension, shock absorbers, tyres and tyre pressures, and the loading of the vehicle, will each have a far reaching effect on its behaviour on corners and bends. The driver's main responsibility is in relation to tyre maintenance. He can exercise some control over tyre conditions and pressures and on the loading of the vehicle, but the other matters are usually in the care of garage workshop staffs.

The Behaviour of a Car when Cornering

5. The problem of driving a car through a curved path is mainly solved by the method of approach. The car cannot negotiate the curve with safety and on the course directed by the driver unless the tyres retain an efficient grip on the road. The whole time a car is in motion under proper control, a portion of the tyre tread is in direct contact with the road and, in theory, there should be no movement of that portion of the tyre relative to the road surface.

6. When a car is driven round a corner certain forces are set up, the amount of which is controlled by the driver, and these tend to overcome the grip of the tyres on the road. The driver will appreciate the significance of these forces by referring to Figure 23, which is in two parts, the lower showing the plan view of a car turning a left-hand corner and the upper showing a rear end elevation of the car in the same situation.

7. The plan view shows three arrows, lettered 'A', 'B' and 'C', which represent powers acting through the centre of gravity of the car. The arrow 'A' represents the momentum of the car, which is proportional to the car's weight and speed. The amount of the momentum will therefore be created by the driver through his control of the car's speed. The direction of momentum will be opposed to the turn to be made. In order to turn the corner the driver turns the steering wheel and directs the front of the car to the left; this directional control is shown on the figure by the arrow 'B'. The combination of the forces 'A' and 'B' directs the course of the car into a circular path which, by the mass weight of the car, creates an outward pull which is known as centrifugal force, shown on the figure by the arrow 'C'.

8. The grip of the tyres on the road must be capable of exercising the necessary inward pull on the car to prevent it slipping outwards under the effect of centrifugal force. If the grip does this the car will follow the curved path directed by the driver; if not, it will slide outwards across the road.

9. To summarise these conditions:

(1) The driver controls the amount of momentum by his speed of approach to the corner.

(2) He turns the car into a circular path by his directional control.

(3) Centrifugal force is thus created, which will pull the car outwards into a skid if the tyres are unable to exert the necessary inward and opposing pull.

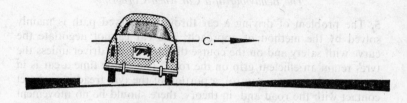

A. Momentum
B. Directional Control
C. Centrifugal Force

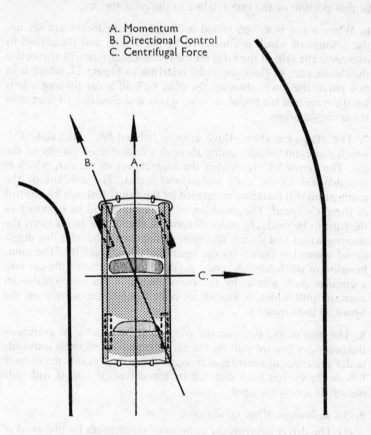

Cornering forces

FIGURE 23

10. The upper part of Figure 23, giving the rear end elevation, shows the behaviour of the car through the vertical axis when it is turning left. As the car turns, the weight tends to build up on the outside wheels, causing the car to heel over. Soft sprung cars, or those with a high centre of gravity, will tend to heel over more than others. In any case, the tyre pressures will be important for, under pressure, tyre walls become excessively flexed, resulting in tyre distortion, which will accentuate the heeling over effect and reduce the power of the tyres to resist centrifugal force.

11. Whilst considering the behaviour of the car about its vertical axis during cornering, it is well to consider what happens if brakes are applied in the corner. As stated above, when the car turns, the weight distribution builds up on the outside wheels. When brakes are applied it is found that weight is thrown forward. It therefore follows that, when brakes are applied in a corner, the outside front wheel will be bearing a considerable weight, with the car tending to pivot on it. Obviously a car under such stress will be more difficult to handle.

The Road Camber or Crossfall

12. The camber or crossfall of the road will also have a bearing on the effect of centrifugal force. A normal camber dropping from the crown of the road to the kerb will prove favourable on left-hand bends and unfavourable on right-hand bends, for the obvious reason that a car slides more easily downhill. Some corners and bends however are super-elevated, that is, the whole width of the road is constructed with a banking in such a way that the crossfall will be favourable to the passage of a car round the bend in either direction.

The System of Car Control for Corners and Bends

13. In order to put to good use the information on cornering contained in the foregoing paragraphs, it is essential that the driver's observation on every corner he has to negotiate shall be of the highest order. His judgment (which will improve with experience) will lead him to apply correct values in his controlling actions on the car. He must recognise every corner as a hazard and consider each feature of the System of Car Control at the approach to it. On a car fitted with automatic transmission which has a device permitting the manual selection of a lower gear and the locking of the transmission in that gear, this device can be operated if it is considered that a gear lower than top is required for the negotiation of this type of hazard.

14. All corners or bends demand the application of the following principles:

    (i) Correct positioning of the car on the approach side. (Course selected.)

    (ii) Right choice of speed. (Mirrors, Signals and Brakes.)

    (iii) Correct gear for the speed. (Gear.)

    (iv) Car to take the corner under the influence of progressive acceleration whenever possible—not rolling round while decelerating or being wrenched round with the brakes on.

By the application of these principles the following safety factors will be apparent as the car is about to leave the bend or corner:

    (a) It will be on the correct side of the road.

    (b) It will be able to remain there.

    (c) It will be able to stop in the distance the driver can see to be clear of other traffic.

Skidding

15. In the first part of this chapter cornering was discussed, and the grip of the tyres on the road was found to be essential if a car is to negotiate corners and bends with safety. It is now proposed to investigate what happens if, unfortunately, the grip of the tyres fails and a skid occurs.

16. Every driver of a motor vehicle on the public highway should aim to drive and control his machine in such a way that skidding never occurs. This is not always possible when the roads are covered with ice or frozen snow, or during bad weather, but it is safe to affirm that many accidents which are alleged to have been due to skidding in ordinary wet weather would never have occurred if the drivers had had a better understanding of the causes of skidding and a better control over their vehicles when in a skid.

17. Preventing, causing and controlling skidding are practical elements in the driving of a motor car, and an hour's practice on a skid pan or on a slippery private road will be more valuable than many hours of talking or reading on the subject. It is possible, however, to give some advice on the theory of the subject which will help the practical effort.

18. Skidding may be defined as follows:

Involuntary movement of the car due to the grip of the tyres on the road becoming less than a force or forces acting on the car. In other words a car skids when one or more wheels slide instead of having a pure rolling action.

The driver should examine this definition and consider the kind of forces which might act on the car and, more important, how they may be created.

19. Any driver who has experienced a skid will realise that he was changing either his speed or his direction immediately before the skid developed. From this it appears that skidding is usually caused by accelerating, braking or changing direction so suddenly or forcibly as to create forces more powerful than the grip between the tyres and the road.

20. Figure 24 shows the plan view of a car. The four arrows, lettered Y1, Y2, Y3 and Y4, illustrate the various forces and their approximate direction of operation which can be controlled by the driver. Y1 and Y2 are the sideways forces, caused by turning to the left or right. Y3 is a retarding force caused by braking and locking the road wheels. Y4 is the acceleration force causing wheel spin. Obviously a driver can create a combination of these forces by braking or accelerating whilst the car is describing a curved path.

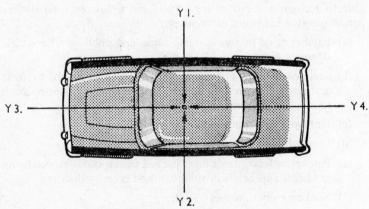

Forces acting on a car in motion

FIGURE 24

21. All these forces will be operating on the car from time to time whilst it is in motion. The important thing to remember is that the driver must not allow them to become so powerful as to overcome the grip of his tyres on the road. The Transport and Road Research Laboratory conduct experiments on the grip value of different types of road surface. For this purpose they use special apparatus which records in graph form a value which they call the Sideway Force Co-efficient. From the driver's point of view (which is more practical than scientific) the most important fact revealed by these experiments is that the grip of a tyre on a road surface is relative to the speed of the vehicle along that surface. Almost every kind of surface has a good grip value when speed is kept low in the region of 5 m.p.h., but as speed increases (and the maximum test speed is 30 m.p.h.) the grip value falls rapidly on some surfaces, notably wood blocks and smooth asphalt. Macadam and concrete surfaces, however, show up very well as speed increases.

TO MINIMISE THE RISK OF SKIDDING

22. The importance of good tyre treads and correct tyre pressures has already been stressed. Any neglect of these will increase the risk of skidding when driving on slippery roads.

23. Every driver should keep a good look out for sections of road surface which are soiled. To realise that the surface is slippery only when the vehicle is running over it is too late. Every driver should be able to recognise ahead of his vehicle the following road surface conditions (the list is not exhaustive):

(a) Patches of oil or grease at cab ranks and public service vehicle stopping places.

(b) Sections of road presenting smooth surfaces caused by wear and impregnation with rubber, dust and oil at the approach to cross-roads, corners and bends.

(c) Unfavourable cambers at corners and bends.

(d) Loose dust or gravel.

(e) Patches of frost, ice or hard-packed frozen snow, especially on gradients and bends in suburban and country districts.

(f) Sunken gullies, man-holes, etc.

24. When such conditions are encountered speed must be reduced. The smoothest control over speed in these conditions will be obtained through the accelerator pedal, which will regulate the speed of the engine and, of course, that of the road wheels through the transmission. Braking, if used, and any alterations to the steering, must be effected with such smoothness and delicacy that tyre adhesion to the road is not impaired.

SKID PAN

25. The ideal type of skid pan is one comprising an area laid with different types of road surface. It should be capable of being marked out into various straight sections and should include several corners.

CAUSES OF SKIDDING

26. To learn to control a skid the driver must learn how skidding is caused. It may be caused by the following, singly or in combination:

    (a) Excessive speed, which is a basic cause.

    (b) Coarse steering in relation to a speed which in itself is not excessive.

    (c) Harsh acceleration.

    (d) Excessive or sudden braking.

CORRECTING A SKID

27. The first requirement for correcting a skid is to know its type and to recognise the sensations transmitted to the driver by the behaviour of the car in the early stages of the skid's development. These sensations should be linked with the manner of control prevailing at the moment of skidding.

SENSATIONS ASSOCIATED WITH SKIDDING

28. *Rear Wheel Skid.*—A rear wheel skid caused by combinations of (a), (b) and (c) in para. 26 gives a sensation of unbalance to the human body produced by the car endeavouring to turn about its vertical axis. The normal feel of the steering is replaced by one of extreme lightness, the car tends to turn broadside and, if unchecked, will tend to turn completely round. A rear wheel skid caused by (d) in para. 26 produces similar sensations, but with the addition that the desired loss of road speed does not take place.

29. *Front Wheel Skid.*—When this occurs, usually on a corner or bend, the sensation is that of complete loss of steering control, the vehicle going straight ahead instead of following the course of the deflected front wheels. The cause undoubtedly arises from excessive speed and/or excessive or sudden braking.

30. *Four-Wheel Skid.*—A four-wheel skid caused by (d) in para. 26 will produce a sensation of increased speed rather than of the desired loss of it, and the car will tend to slide forward.

31. *Guiding Principles for Correcting Skidding.*—Immediately the sensation of skidding is felt, it is imperative that the driver exercises a controlling influence over the vehicle or the skid will develop to alarming proportions. The following notes are given as guiding principles, but practice in the art is essential.

32. (1) *Rear Wheel Skid* caused by (a), (b) or (c) in para. 26. Eliminate the cause by removing pressure on the accelerator pedal. At the same moment turn the front wheels INTO the skid—or, in other words, if the rear of the car swings to the right, turn the steering wheel to the right until stabilisation is achieved; similarly, if the rear of the car swings to the left, steer in that direction. Then steer into the desired course and apply gentle acceleration. Excessive or prolonged steering correction should be avoided, or another skid may be induced in the opposite direction.

(2) *Front Wheel Skid* caused by (a) or (d) in para. 26. Eliminate the cause by removing the pressure on the accelerator pedal or brake pedal and, at the same moment, straighten the front wheels.

(3) *Four-Wheel Skid* caused by (d) in para. 26. Eliminate the cause immediately by stopping braking momentarily to allow the road wheels to rotate. Then re-apply brakes with a delicate initial pressure which may be increased gradually, so as to avoid locking the wheels again.

CONCLUSIONS ON SKIDDING

33. Every experienced driver knows, and every learner driver will find by experience, that concentration and quick reaction play a highly important part in driving on slippery roads without skidding. If a skid does occur, these same human qualities will be indispensable in the correction and control of the car. It has been previously mentioned, and is here stressed again, that the best control over the speed of a car on a slippery road is through the accelerator pedal.

This is only possible through the clutch and a suitable gear ratio. So the driver is advised that, when controlling a skid on an average private car, it is generally best to leave the clutch engaged. If speed is excessive, normal braking is not advised, but if a lower gear is within road speed range a quick change down may be effected to reduce road speed. In this case, when the lower gear is engaged, great care must be taken to ensure smooth transmission of engine power through the clutch to the road wheels. On cars fitted with automatic transmission recourse should never be made to the use of the ' kick-down ' method of engaging a lower gear as this will certainly induce wheel spin and cause a skid. Instead, the device for manually engaging and holding a lower gear should be used.

The instruction on skidding is given for three reasons:

(1) To raise the standard of driving to the highest degree of all-round efficiency;

(2) To give confidence in driving under any conditions; and

(3) To equip the driver to meet any emergency which might arise.

It must be clearly understood that in no circumstances should skidding be practised on a public road.

34. The following paragraphs apply mainly to gear changing on a car fitted with a conventional manually operated gearbox. Gear changing on a car fitted with automatic transmission will normally occur according to the speed of the car and the throttle position, so that wear and tear is reduced to the minimum and there is always sufficient power being developed by the engine. There are circumstances when over-riding manual control is desirable, and these are dealt with under the appropriate subject headings in the Manual.

Gear Changing

35. One of the most admirable qualities to be found in the good driver is ability to make the best use of the gear ratios of the car he is driving. Gear changing in itself is not a difficult operation. On most modern cars easy gear change devices automatically smooth out the difficulties which were experienced by drivers of the earlier cars which were fitted with plain ' crash ' gearboxes.

36. Notwithstanding the modern gear change devices, it is still considered beneficial that the driver should use the double de-clutching method of changing gear.

37. The following paragraphs aim to improve the driver's knowledge and judgment of the correct use of the gears available to him on the average car fitted with a four-speed gearbox. To this end he must have a good knowledge of the main components of the gearbox and their function when the accelerator, clutch or gear lever is moved.

38. It is through the gearbox that the power of the engine is transmitted to the road wheels. The power available is limited and is proportional to the r.p.m. of the engine. Therefore different gears are used to make it possible for the engine to maintain r.p.m. and perform the work necessary to move the car from stationary, accelerate, decelerate and travel along the road, up and down hill, at any safe speed up to the car's maximum.

MOVING FROM STATIONARY AND CHANGING UP

39. A car may be put into motion smoothly and its speed increased progressively without undue stress on the engine or transmission if the gearbox is properly used. The following procedure should therefore be followed:

(1) Get the car rolling in first gear to overcome its inertia, then change up to second gear.

(2) Accelerate in second gear, then change into third gear.

(3) Accelerate in third gear, then change into top gear.

By this method the speed of the car will be increased smoothly, and briskly if necessary, and maximum road speed may be achieved as quickly as possible if this is desired. Care must be taken not to ' over-rev ' in an intermediate gear.

CHANGING DOWN

40. From the previous paragraph it is obvious that as speed increases to a certain limit in each gear so a change up is effected; on the other hand, when a car's speed is reduced, by the severity of a gradient or because it must slow down on account of traffic conditions, a lower gear must be selected to supply the power required either to climb the hill or to effect the smooth turning effort which is necessary for slow progress in traffic.

41. Ability in judging when to change down to a lower gear is a very practical part of the training of a driver.

42. Occasions for a change to a lower gear may be recognised in the following signs and symptoms:

(a) A loss of road speed coupled with a reduction of engine r.p.m. and loss of reserve of power.

(b) The increasing difficulty of road conditions observed ahead, such as the severity of a gradient, the slow movement of traffic proceeding ahead, or the approach to a hazard.

43. The selection of a suitable lower gear at the correct time will provide the advantages which are desirable in the following road circumstances.

(a) On an up gradient, to maintain the power to climb the hill without undue loss of speed or engine r.p.m.

(b) At the approach to a hazard, to enable the driver to accelerate out of the hazard if this is safe, or to stop more readily if necessary.

(c) When travelling at low speeds or when in doubt about traffic conditions ahead, to provide the reserve of power and flexibility to accelerate or decelerate by control through the accelerator pedal.

(d) On a slippery road, when the use of engine compression to lose speed is safer than braking, since the latter would be liable to cause skidding.

(e) On a steep down gradient, to control speed with engine compression, thereby avoiding long periods of hard braking.

In the conditions described in this paragraph on a car fitted with automatic transmission which has a device for manually selecting and holding a lower gear, this can be used to achieve the desired control.

44. No matter how well a driver may handle a car, his ability to use the gearbox properly will do much to make or mar his driving. The first-class driver should aim always:

(a) To be in the correct gear for every road speed and traffic condition.

(b) To make all gear changes quietly.

(c) After selecting the gear, to connect the engine power to the transmission without jerk or jar to the machine.

(d) To be capable of engaging a particular gear without first using an intermediate gear.

(e) To know the approximate maximum road speed of the car he is driving in the intermediate gears.

(f) To avoid changing gear when alongside a vehicle it is over-taking (both hands should remain on the steering wheel).

45. To satisfy these requirements the driver should endeavour to improve his ability to judge road speed without reference to the speedometer and to judge engine r.p.m. by sound in each gear at various speeds. He should pay great attention to the details of the precise manipulation of the accelerator, clutch and gear lever. If at first he is not as successful as he expects to be, he should take frequent spells of practice, concentrating on gear changing alone.

CONCLUSIONS ON GEAR CHANGING

46. Car sympathy is a quality to be admired in any driver. It is shown in many ways, not the least of which is the manipulation of the gear changing controls and the r.p.m. used in any gear.

47. The handling of the average car engine can be heard and felt, and the knowledge gained by the combined use of these senses should enable the driver to drive his car with that delicacy and smoothness, sometimes called ' polish ', which is so much admired amongst keen motorists.

48. Some common faults when changing gear with a conventional manually operated gearbox, and in its kindred operations, are set out below:

(1) Failure to appreciate the basic working principles of the main components of the gearbox, *i.e.* main-shaft and lay-shaft, and their behaviour under various running conditions.

(2) Inability to recognise the sound of engine speed, and the correct relationship between it and the road speed of the car.

(3) Failure to assess road speed correctly before selecting a particular gear. The commonest error is that of trying to engage second gear at too high a speed.

(4) Failure to take a proper grip on the gear lever when moving it from one position to another. This is the root of many gear changing difficulties.

(5) Lack of precise co-ordination between foot and hand movements to effect a clean, smooth gear change.

(6) Late gear changing, or entire failure to change down, at the approach to a hazard when the road speed and conditions demand a lower gear.

(7) Failure to recognise the sound of the engine when ' over-revving ' in a low gear. This fault is often associated with the act of overtaking.

(8) Timidity and reluctance to attempt necessary changes down to low gears after previous unsuccessful attempts.

49. Some common faults when driving cars fitted with automatic transmission are set out below:

(1) Engaging ' D ' with a high revving engine, the foot not being clear of the accelerator pedal.

(2) Attempting to ' kick-down ' on approach to hazards with the result that the car is travelling too fast, making it necessary to apply secondary and often harsh braking.

(3) Engaging ' L ' at too high a road speed.

(4) Moving the selector to ' N ' when making temporary stops in traffic and then engaging ' D ' with the foot not clear of the accelerator pedal.

(5) Braking with the left foot when stopping, the driver being used to depressing the clutch when stopping with a conventional gearbox.

(6) Not maintaining pressure on the accelerator pedal after ' kicking-down ' when overtaking, resulting in top gear being engaged before the overtaking has been completed.

(7) Engaging ' L ' when accelerating from stationary and then engaging ' D ' at 30 m.p.h. This is a bad fault and puts unnecessary stress on the transmission.

(8) On the type of transmission which has a quadrant 'L.D.N.R.P.', engaging 'L' and accelerating to maximum speed then moving the selector to ' D ' and overshooting into ' N ' and then back to ' D ' with maximum engine revolutions. This causes serious damage to the front clutch transmission.

F

CHAPTER 7

The Use of Speed

1. In this age, speed of movement has become an important factor in our daily lives. Designers of cars are paying more attention each year to acceleration. They recognise quite rightly that there is safety in the ability to accelerate rapidly. At the same time capacity to maintain high road speeds takes a forward place in modern design, particularly in view of the introduction of special roads for fast traffic.

2. Speed is frequently looked upon as something dangerous in itself, but it is dangerous only if used in the wrong place or at the wrong time. It does, however, impose a heavy responsibility on the shoulders of the motorist. He is in control of machinery which can be as lethal as a loaded firearm if it is not handled with the utmost care and common sense. His speed must at all times be adjusted to suit the prevailing circumstances, including weather, road, traffic and other conditions.

3. Statutory restrictions on speed with reference to area and classes of vehicles have been applied for the preservation of public safety. Their value in that cause has already been demonstrated, but statutory limits are not in themselves sufficient. Many instances of dangerous or careless driving occur at speeds below those limits.

4. It is a driver's duty—with his own knowledge of the safe use of speed—to guard carefully against dangerous and careless driving at low speeds as well as high, remembering that speed is relative and that at one time and place a higher speed may be safe and a lower speed dangerous, but a short distance farther on that situation may be reversed.

5. His own ability to drive at speed with safety depends initially upon a sound knowledge and practical application of the principles set out in earlier chapters, in particular those dealing with the System of Car Control, road observation and the proper use of the horn. His mental alertness must never flag. He must be ready for any emergency and able to sense hidden danger. Physical fitness, moreover, is all important if mental concentration is to be kept at the high pitch needed for fast driving.

6. The effect of speed on vision has been dealt with in a previous chapter, but the subject being closely related to the proper use of speed, needs further mention here. Travelling slowly, a driver's attention is directed to things in the immediate foreground, and at speed to more distant things. His eyes automatically vary their focus according to his speed.

7. For example, an object at the side of the road will automatically be noted by a driver travelling at a slow speed, but not at 50 or 60 miles an hour, because objects in the foreground then become blurred or are not seen at all. This is explained by the fact that the eyes have increased their range and become focused on more sharply defined things further ahead. Vision is, so to speak, channelled in much the same way as it is through binoculars.

8. At speed, features of a cottage in the distance (ivy covered, gabled windows, etc.) are plainly discerned. The driver has the illusion that the cottage is travelling towards him and as he nears it his speed of approach quickens, until at the last moment it flashes past and no detail of it can be distinguished. At this stage the eyes have no time to focus themselves on the near objects which, in any case, are at an oblique angle to the driver's vision. Quite definitely, therefore, the farther away an object is when one is travelling at speed, the easier it is to focus one's vision on it.

9. The same principle accounts for the illusion that one is travelling faster along a narrow road than along a wide one. A speed of 30 m.p.h. along a country lane with bordering hedges will seem faster than 50 m.p.h. on, say, a dual carriageway. This is explained by the fact that the hedges in the lane are close to the car and are, in consequence, difficult to focus, apart from which the reverberation of noise due to the shut-in nature of the road adds to the impression of speed. On motorways, dual carriageways and other fast trunk roads, however, the boundaries are more distant from the carriageway with intervening stretches of grass. Thus, the nearest objects, being some distance away, can be more easily focused and are too remote to reflect the sounds made by the car.

10. It must also be borne in mind that the senses may be deceived by vibration and judgment confused by noises within the car. Take as a very simple example the contrast between driving a car with a

F*

noisy engine, rattling windows, etc., and one of quality. With the former one gets the impression that it is travelling faster than its true speed and with the other that its speed is slower than it really is. In consequence, the driver of the quieter vehicle, before changing course into a side road, will find himself approaching the corner much faster than he estimates.

11. Again, the bumpiness, lurching and swaying of a badly sprung car inducing general discomfort to the occupants, gives them the impression of high speed.

12. So, too, with night driving the apparent speed is greater than the actual. A speed of, say, 30 m.p.h. seems faster than the same speed in daylight. One must remember that there is a limit to the range within which one's headlamps can illuminate forward points sufficiently to bring them clearly within one's vision and it is a maxim that a driver's speed should always be such that he can pull up within that range, *i.e.*, a distance within which he has a clear field of vision.

13. Physical endurance is an important factor in fast driving. However fit a driver may be he is bound to undergo severe mental and physical strain when maintaining high speeds over considerable distances, frequently over unfamiliar roads. He must concentrate the whole time and be ever alert for the emergency. It is inevitable, therefore, that he will experience a feeling of fatigue accompanied by eye strain, and when this occurs he would be wise to hand over the wheel to a colleague or at least to stop for a ' breather '. Fatigue increases the risk of accidents.

14. If called on to drive a strange car a driver should realise that he cannot with safety drive it as fast as one to which he is accustomed. However comfortable he may feel in the driving seat, his controlling movements, particularly in an emergency, will be noticeably slower and even prone to misjudgment if the controls (brake and gear levers, etc.) are slightly differently placed. Its road holding, accelerating and braking powers may be different. The driver's view to the rear may be more restricted. All these things must be borne in mind when at the wheel of a strange car.

15. Efficiency in driving at speed is not easily acquired. It needs study throughout one's driving life. When circumstances make it necessary to drive at high speed it is of vital importance to remember and put into practice all that has been set out earlier in this Manual about concentration, steering, braking, cornering, etc. At 30 m.p.h. a minor driving error can probably be rectified. At 70 m.p.h. the same error can have disastrous consequences.

16. To sum up:

(1) Don't drive at high speeds unless it is safe to do so.

(2) Don't relax for an instant. Use all your skill and power of concentration.

(3) Always drive so that you can pull up within the range of your vision whether by day or by night.

(4) Remember if you double your speed you quadruple your braking distance.

(5) Don't be misled as to your speed by noises (within or outside the car) or vibration.

(6) Put into practice all the principles covered in earlier chapters.

(7) Guard against fatigue.

CHAPTER 8

Motorway Driving

Object of Chapter

1. The object of this chapter is to ensure that the driver realises that motorways are different from normal roads, but by keeping to the principles laid down in previous chapters he will be able to ensure the high degree of safety, which is of paramount importance, having regard to the high speeds encountered on motorways.

2. The design and purpose of motorways is to provide a safe and unhindered passage along main transport routes. They provide an opportunity to maintain higher average speeds than on normal roads. This is achieved by eliminating or reducing the more usual sources of danger, such as two-way traffic, cross-traffic, traffic lights, and also prohibiting certain classes of road user.

3. Motorways in themselves vary in design, some sections having three-lane carriageways, whereas others have only two lanes. Each carriageway is separated by a central reservation of varying widths and make-up—some incorporating crash barriers, mesh fencing or planted hedgerows. On the nearside of each carriageway is an easily distinguishable hard shoulder for use in an emergency or breakdown.

Entering the Motorway

4. Before entering the motorway the driver should have particular regard to the fitness of his vehicle and himself, as dealt with in previous chapters. Any failure on his part in this respect may lead to vehicle breakdown, driver fatigue, and the possibility of an accident.

5. The approach roads to any motorway are clearly marked with the distinctive blue signs, and it is essential that the correct carriageway is entered. Know where you are going and at what point you should leave the motorway in order to reach your intended destination.

6. Traffic will always join a motorway from a slip road on the left. A slip road has two lanes, but the driver should avoid being in the lane adjacent to the motorway when reaching the motorway proper, because the acceleration lane on the left of the motorway has room for only one line of traffic. Full use of the acceleration lane should be made by the driver in varying the speed of his vehicle so that he can merge safely with traffic already using the motorway.

7. It must be clearly understood that a driver should be prepared to give way, and if necessary stop, on the acceleration lane, if he cannot merge safely without impeding traffic already using the motorway. After entering the left-hand lane, the driver should accustom himself to road and traffic conditions before he considers using the road to full advantage.

On the Motorway

8. Having considered and appreciated the road surface, weather and traffic conditions, together with the type of vehicle being used, the driver should decide upon a speed well within the capabilities of his car, himself, any speed limits and prevailing traffic conditions. He should aim at a fairly constant speed, bearing in mind that an occasional variation may be beneficial both to the driver and the vehicle.

9. Monotony in motorway driving can be exaggerated by keeping the engine noise or vehicle speed at too steady a pitch. This will cause a constant drumming noise, which can induce an effect of hypnosis, with the attendant inability to react with the necessary precision in an emergency.

10. It has been found beneficial to close the windows of the car when joining the motorway to reduce both noise and drag. Hand signals at speed are unnecessary and dangerous. However, adequate ventilation is essential to avoid drowsiness and fatigue; these are real sources of danger in motorway driving.

11. It will be found that a horn warning as such, when given at high speeds, is generally ineffective. In view of this most car manufacturers are now incorporating a switch, within easy reach of the driver, which operates the main beam of the headlights. This can be used to good effect to warn other motorists about to be overtaken. It should be given sufficiently early for the other driver to be able to react to the signal.

12. It can be stressed here that care should be taken to avoid excessive flashing; this could create an impression of aggressiveness to vehicles being overtaken and it could also dazzle oncoming traffic.

13. When considering a suitable speed thought should be given to the type and condition of the tyres fitted to the car, including their pressures. The possibility of tyre failure should be constantly borne in mind when travelling at sustained high speeds. A careful and continual check must be kept on all instruments and gauges to ensure correct functioning of all engine parts and auxiliary equipment. In addition, a check should be made of the windscreen wipers and washers, if fitted, to ensure they are working correctly. Mud and spray is frequently thrown up by other vehicles using the motorway and if not removed this dirt can seriously affect visibility. Opportunity should be taken at suitable intervals to clean the headlights. Mud and spray will build up on these and reduce their effectiveness.

14. A dangerous situation can often develop on a motorway when vehicles bunch closely together travelling at the same speed. Care should be exercised when this is encountered, and it is advisable to hold well back until the situation resolves itself and the overtaking manœuvre can be carried out with perfect safety.

15. Danger can arise when catching up with a group of slower moving vehicles, which themselves are closing on each other. Here again it is as well to hold back and let the other traffic sort itself out before overtaking. If this is overlooked one can easily find oneself alongside a vehicle which is in the act of pulling out, often without any signal, and being forced off the road.

16. The advice given in the Highway Code in relation to lane discipline must be strictly adhered to. It is important to stress the need to keep to the proper driving lane, keeping a frequent check on the driving mirror so that when any variance of speed or lane is contemplated the state of following traffic is known and appreciated.

17. An adequate distance should always be kept between a vehicle and the one in front, bearing in mind the braking distances generally accepted, and how these can be affected by adverse road conditions, such as heavy rain, snow or ice, etc. It is possible, of course, that on a long distance journey on a motorway, when there is little or no need to apply the brakes, there could be a seepage of water into the brake linings, and care should be taken to test them occasionally when using the motorway in this type of weather to avoid failure in an emergency.

18. Because of the higher average speeds used and encountered on motorways, it is necessary to look as far ahead as possible so that any necessary deviation in course can be made in good time. A constant watch should be kept on the road surface for any obstruction or other material which may have fallen from other vehicles. Various types of debris will be encountered, and striking any object at speed can cause damage to tyres and other vehicle parts.

19. Emergency traffic signs should be strictly complied with. The signs are placed with road safety in mind, and when seen a definite easing of speed is necessary so that the driver can get a clear and early view of the hazard he is approaching.

20. Any deviation in course should be signalled well in advance and, if it can be safely carried out, commenced early and continued gradually. An early signal and gradual deviation will allow time for following traffic to respond to the changing situation or, alternatively, for a driver intending such a movement, to leave himself time and sufficient distance to revert to his previous course, should something untoward develop.

21. Speed should be increased when overtaking to enable the manœuvre to be carried out as quickly and safely as possible. Signal the intention if necessary, and position well beforehand to achieve a view past the vehicle/s to be overtaken.

Weather Conditions

22. Weather conditions have a direct bearing on visibility and road holding. It cannot be stressed too strongly that one should always drive so that one can stop in the distance seen to be clear of other traffic. In fog and heavy rain when visibility is reduced, speed must also be reduced drastically to keep within the bounds of safety.

23. Heavy rain lying on the road surface is a further hazard when driving at speed. It builds up in the form of a wedge between the tyres and the road surface, and the wheels cease revolving and instead, slide over the watery surface. This is termed ' aqua-planing '. When it happens, complete loss of control is rapid and, to combat it, speed must be reduced to enable the tyres to re-establish their grip on the road.

24. The design of motorways is such that they are often on a higher level than the surrounding countryside. In consequence they are more prone to the effects of high winds. These are often apparent when leaving a cutting or entering or emerging from under bridges and going into open country. On windy days care should be taken when overtaking large heavy vehicles; these tend to act as windbreaks and one is likely to encounter a heavy buffeting on clearing the front of the vehicle.

25. Never stop on the motorway proper, unless you are obliged to in an emergency or breakdown, but if you have to do so, every effort should be made to get the car off the carriageway as quickly as possible. NOTE: The starter motor of the car, together with a suitably low gear, can be used for this purpose.

Night Driving

26. It is perhaps opportune to bring to mind again Chapter 4, paras. 43 to 46, which refer to night driving, having particular regard to dazzle. Because of their construction, it is possible to have a considerable stretch of straight road, and the consequence of this is that drivers can be dazzled or can cause dazzle for a long period. Avoid dazzling others and, if subjected to it, slow down so that you are able to stop in the distance you can see to be clear, in this case the range of your headlights. Do not drive on when blinded by oncoming traffic. It is far better to train your eyes to look to the left of the lights rather than straight at them.

Leaving the Motorway

27. Signs are placed at one mile and half-mile intervals in advance of the exit point of motorways. A system of chevron indicators at 300-, 200- and 100-yard intervals gives warning of the deceleration lane.

28. Watch for the signs warning you of the approach of your point of exit when you wish to leave the motorway at an intermediate exit point. Get into the left-hand lane in plenty of time, remain in it, and give a left-hand trafficator not later than the 300-yard chevron post. Enter the deceleration lane and use this lane to lose any unwanted road speed.

29. If you miss your exit point you must continue along the motorway until the next one.

After Leaving the Motorway

30. When you leave the motorway, remember to adjust your driving to the differing conditions of the ordinary road system. After a period of high speed driving a speed of 40 m.p.h. may appear almost a crawl. Even the most experienced driver will need to check his speedometer to become aware of his true speed. IT IS VERY NECESSARY TO REMIND ONESELF THAT ONE WILL BE MEETING TWO-WAY TRAFFIC.

Printed in England for Her Majesty's Stationery Office
by McCorquodale Printers Ltd., London

HM 6616   Dd.504338   K880   5/74   McC.   3309

NOTES